Mastering Cybersecurity Excellence

Securing the future beyond cyberthreats.

by Patrick Justus, Ph.D.

Copyright © 2024 Patrick Justus

Contact the author:

pcjustus@gmail.com

Self-published and printed by Amazon KDP.

Printed in the United Kingdom.

Contents

Acknowledgements 6

About the Author 7

Preface 8

Chapter 1: Foundations of Cybersecurity 10

   1. Introduction 10

   1.1 Concept of Cybersecurity 11

      1.1.1 Key Principles of Security - Similarities 11

      1.1.2 Key Differences 12

      1.1.3 Confidentiality, Integrity, Availability (CIA) Triad 13

      1.1.4 Cybersecurity Terminologies 15

      1.1.5 What is Cybersecurity? 19

      1.1.6 The Vital Role of Cybersecurity 20

      1.1.7 Types of Cyber Threats 21

      1.1.8 Cyber Attack Response Plans 24

      1.1.9 Importance of Cybersecurity 27

      1.1.10 Consequences and Implications of Inadequate Cybersecurity 29

   1.2 Understand Core Terminology and Key Aspects of Cybersecurity 33

      1.2.1 Define Core Terminologies (Technologies) Used in Cybersecurity 33

      1.2.2 Explain the Terms Good Actors and Bad Actors 34

      1.2.3 Distinguish Typical Behaviours of Good Actors and Bad Actors 35

      1.2.4 Grey Hat Hackers: Bridging the Divide 36

      1.2.5 Types of Threat Actors: Understanding Motivations and Objectives 37

      1.2.6 Motivations of Good and Bad Actors in Cybersecurity 38

      1.2.7 Key Vulnerable Sectors in Cybersecurity 39

      1.2.8 Motivations for Cyber-Attacks Across Key Sectors 41

      1.2.9 The Cyber Kill Chain: Understanding the Stages of a Cyber-Attack 42

1.3 Security by Design Principles 44
1.3.1 Principles of Security by Design 44
1.3.2 Consequences of Neglecting Cybersecurity in the Design Phase 45
1.3.3 Evaluation of Security by Design 46
1.4 The Human Element in Cybersecurity 47
1.5 The Cybersecurity Landscape Today: Navigating Complexity and Innovation 48

Chapter 2: Navigating Cybersecurity Frameworks 50
2. Introduction 51
2.1 Understand Cyber Threat Intelligence 52
2.1.1 Key Aspects of Cyber Threat Intelligence (CTI) 52
2.1.2 Describe the Threat Intelligence Lifecycle 54
2.1.3 Unearthing Emerging Attack Techniques 56
2.1.4 Open-Source Intelligence (OSINT) Data Sets 58
2.1.5 The Imperative of Reliable OSINT Sources 60
2.1.6 Practical Guidelines and Best Practices 61
2.1.7 The Anchoring Role of Reliable Sources 62
2.1.8 Current Threat Status and Recommendations 64
2.1.9 General Recommendations to Enhance Cybersecurity Posture 64
2.1.10 Tailoring Intelligence for Your Organisation 66
2.2 Understand Threat Models 69
2.2.1 The Essence of Threat Modelling 69
2.2.2 Identifying Vulnerabilities and Assets 73
2.3 Evaluating Risk and Prioritising Defences 74
2.3 Understand Malicious Software 77
2.3.1 Categories of Malicious Software 77
2.3.2 Techniques and Tactics of Malicious Software 78
2.3.3 Detecting and Mitigating Malware 79
2.3.4 Case Studies: Notorious Malware Attacks 80

2.4 Knowing About Social Engineering 82
2.4.1 The Psychology of Social Engineering 82
2.4.2 Common Social Engineering Techniques 85
2.4.3 Defending Against Social Engineering Attacks 86

Chapter 3: Upholding Cybersecurity Governance and Compliance 89
3. About this chapter 90
3.1.1: Understand Common Types of Testing in Cybersecurity 91
3.1.2 Identify Why Cybersecurity Testing Is Important 92
3.1.3 Compare Types of Cybersecurity Testing 93
3.1.4 Consider Mitigations Following Cybersecurity Testing 94
3.1.5 Why Is It Important to Retest Following Any Changes Made 95
3.1.6 How the Outcomes of Cybersecurity Testing Can Be Reported 96
3.1.7 Why Outcomes Must Be Reported: 97
Quiz: Reporting Outcomes of Cybersecurity Testing 98
3.2 Reduce or Remove Potential Cybersecurity Vulnerability 98
3.2.1 Identify Cybersecurity Vulnerabilities 98
3.2.2 Demonstrate the Steps to Be Taken When a Vulnerability Has Been Identified 99
3.2.3 Apply the Correct Response to the Vulnerability 100
3.2.4 Develop an Appropriate Communication to Mitigate Future Vulnerabilities 101
3.3 Understand Controls in Cybersecurity 103
3.3.1 Identify Cybersecurity Controls 103
3.3.2 Basic Cybersecurity Framework 105
3.3.3 Evaluate a Cybersecurity Framework 106
3.4 Applying Cybersecurity Controls 109
3.4.1 How to apply cybersecurity controls. 109
3.4.2 Implement a basic cybersecurity control. 110
3.4.3 Justify the implementation of the chosen cybersecurity control. 111
3.4.4 Why a cybersecurity control might not be applied. 112

Chapter 4: Managing Cybersecurity Operations 114

4. About this chapter 115

4.1. Understanding Cybersecurity Incident Response Plan (CIRP) 116

4.1.1 What is Cybersecurity Incident Response Plan? 117

4.1.2 Describe the circumstances under which a cybersecurity incident response plan is implemented and provide an example. 118

4.1.3 Describe the stages of a cybersecurity incident response lifecycle. 119

4.2 Develop the capability to mitigate or eliminate potential cybersecurity vulnerabilities. 121

4.2.1 Why is it important to maintain an up-to-date cybersecurity incident log. 121

4.2.2 Outline the procedures to incorporate into a cybersecurity incident response plan. 121

4.2.3 What is the significance of having a cybersecurity incident response plan? 122

4.2.4 Develop a cybersecurity incident response plan for an organisation. 123

4.3 Be able to develop an incident post-mortem report. 128

4.3.1 What is an incident post-mortem? 128

4.3.2 The structure of an incident post-mortem. 128

4.3.3 The importance of integrity, rigour and discipline when carrying out an incident 129

4.3.4 Create a post-mortem report of an incident. 129

4.3.5 Reflect upon the post-mortem report and make recommendations based on the findings. 133

4.4 Integrating SMART, SWOT Techniques. 135

Chapter 5: Cybersecurity: Legislation, Trends, and Ethical Considerations 138

5. About this chapter 138

5.1 Understand legislation relating to cyber security. 139

5.1.1 Legislation as it impacts on cybersecurity. 139

5.1.2 Trends in international law for cyberspace. 145

5.2 Introduction to ISO Standards and Their Role in Cybersecurity 148

5.2.1 Key ISO Standards Related to Cybersecurity 149

5.2.2 How ISO Standards Support Cybersecurity 150

5.3 Understanding Ethical Conduct within Cybersecurity 151

5.3.1 Describe Ethical Conduct within Cybersecurity 151

5.3.2 Identify Unethical Conduct within Cybersecurity 152

Chapter 6: Mastering Professional Skills in Cybersecurity 156

6. About this chapter 156

6.1 Understand behaviours required for a career in cybersecurity. 158

6.1.1 Importance of Managing and Promoting a Positive Digital Identity 160

6.1.2 Employee Screening Checks that an Employer Might Carry Out 163

6.1.3 Consequences of Unsatisfactory Findings as a Result of Employer Checks 166

6.1.4 Security Clearance Levels 169

6.1.5 How Bias Can Influence Cybersecurity 172

6.1.6 Benefits of a Security by Design Mindset 174

6.2.1 Skills Required for a Career in Cybersecurity 177

6.2.2 Performing a Personal Skills Analysis 180

6.2.3 Differentiate between SWOT and SOAR analysis 183

6.2.4 Assess own skills against those required for a career in cyber security. 184

6.2.5 Create a Personal Development Plan 189

6.3 Continuous Professional Development (CPD) 192

6.3.1 Key Principles of CPD 192

6.3.2 Benefits of CPD 193

6.3.3 Methods of Keeping Up to Date with Industry Knowledge 194

6.3.4 Importance of Keeping Continuous Professional Development (CPD) Up to Date
.... 196

Acknowledgements

I extend my deepest gratitude to those who have played a significant role in the creation of "Mastering Cybersecurity Excellence." This journey would not have been possible without the unwavering support and encouragement from various corners of my life.

First and foremost, I express my sincere thanks to my former employer, Twin Employment & Training UK, for providing me with the invaluable opportunity to teach cybersecurity remotely to a diverse group of students. Your trust in my abilities has been a driving force behind the insights shared in this book.

To my students, who have been a constant source of inspiration – thank you for your curiosity, engagement, and challenging questions. Your enthusiasm for mastering cybersecurity has fuelled the passion behind these pages.

A special appreciation goes to my daughter, Juanita, who is pursuing her master's degree in Cybercrime & Digital Investigations. Her dedication to the field, insightful feedback, and meticulous editing have significantly enriched the content of this book. Your support has been a pillar of strength throughout this endeavour.

I am profoundly grateful to my loving family for their patience, understanding, and unwavering encouragement during the long hours and countless nights spent writing. Your sacrifices and belief in me have been the bedrock upon which this book stands.

This work is a testament to the collective effort of a supportive network, and I extend my heartfelt thanks to everyone who has been a part of this enriching journey.

With gratitude,

Patrick Justus, Ph.D.

About the Author

Patrick Justus is a distinguished educator, seasoned cybersecurity professional, and the author of the enlightening book, "Mastering Cybersecurity Excellence." With a rich background in Information Systems and Network Security, Dr Justus holds a Ph.D. in the field. His academic qualifications include a B.Sc. (Hons.) in Software Engineering and an M.Sc. in Distributed Computing Systems. He's an alumnus of the University of East London and the University of Greenwich.

Bringing over three decades of experience as a Grade 1 Teacher, Patrick seamlessly transitioned into teaching the Level 5 Diploma in Education & Training, enriching the learning experiences of countless students. His extensive tenure as a Computer Science and ICT teacher, coupled with certifications as a teacher, assessor, and internal verifier, underscores his commitment to education.

As a Head of ICT & Network Manager at the British Nigerian Academy in Nigeria and later as Operations & IT Director for Emco Oilfield Services Ltd., Patrick played pivotal roles in managing network security infrastructures and directing corporate IT initiatives. His leadership extended to academia, where he served as the Head of ICT at WLCBMS HE College, contributing to curriculum development, quality assurance and staff training.

In "Mastering Cybersecurity Excellence," Patrick Justus distils his vast knowledge and practical insights into a comprehensive guide for cybersecurity professionals and enthusiasts alike. The book reflects his commitment to staying at the forefront of technological advancements, evident in his numerous certifications and continuous professional development.

Beyond the realms of academia and cybersecurity, Patrick is a member of the British Computer Society (MBCS). His passion for teaching extends into his book, where he not only imparts technical knowledge but also emphasizes the importance of effective leadership and management in the ever-evolving landscape of cybersecurity.

"Mastering Cybersecurity Excellence" stands as a testament to Patrick Justus's dedication to education, cybersecurity, and the continuous pursuit of excellence. His ability to seamlessly blend academic rigour with real-world experience makes this book an invaluable resource for professionals, students, and anyone seeking to navigate the complexities of cybersecurity with confidence and expertise.

Preface

Welcome to a comprehensive journey through the intricate realm of cybersecurity in this meticulously crafted book. With an insightful blend of theoretical foundations, practical strategies, and professional development guidance, this book stands as a beacon for individuals seeking to excel in the dynamic and ever-evolving field of cybersecurity.

Chapter 1: Foundations of Cybersecurity Embark on your cybersecurity odyssey with a solid foundation. Chapter 1 unravels the fundamental concepts, providing a robust understanding of cybersecurity principles, threat landscapes, and the imperative role of ethical considerations. The Chapter also unravels the latest trends in cybersecurity. From artificial intelligence to the Internet of Things, exploring cutting-edge technologies and their impact on the evolving cybersecurity landscape.

Chapter 2: Navigating Cybersecurity Frameworks Navigate the intricate tapestry of cybersecurity frameworks. Chapter 2 intricately examines prominent frameworks, empowering readers to choose and implement strategies that align seamlessly with industry standards and organisational needs.

Chapter 3: Upholding Cybersecurity Governance and Compliance Dive into the critical realms of governance and compliance in Chapter 3. Uncover the strategic approaches to designing effective cybersecurity governance structures and ensuring compliance with regulatory requirements, covering topics related to testing, vulnerability management, controls, and the application of controls, securing the very fabric of organisational resilience.

Chapter 4: Managing Cybersecurity Operations Elevate your operational prowess in Chapter 4. This chapter delves into the tactical aspects of cybersecurity operations, exploring incident response, threat intelligence, and the practical application of security measures to fortify organisational defences.

Chapter 5: Cybersecurity: Legislation, Trends, and Ethical Considerations delves into the impact of legislation, using examples like the Computer Misuse Act and GDPR. It explores international trends, highlighting collaborative efforts like the EU's data protection approach. The chapter emphasizes ISO standards' role, including ISO/IEC 27001 and ISO/IEC 27032, in fortifying cybersecurity globally. Ethical considerations are detailed, covering principles guiding responsible conduct and identifying unethical behaviours. In essence, the chapter provides a nuanced understanding of legal, international, and ethical frameworks in cybersecurity.

Chapter 6: Mastering Professional Skills in Cybersecurity Culminate your journey with a holistic exploration of professional skills and behaviour. Chapter 6 not only outlines the technical and soft skills requisite for success in cybersecurity but also provides a roadmap for personal development, strategic planning, and continuous professional growth.

This book is a compass for professionals at all stages of their cybersecurity journey. Whether you're a novice seeking foundational knowledge or a seasoned expert aiming to stay ahead, each chapter offers unique insights, practical strategies, and a roadmap for navigating the complex terrain of cybersecurity. Prepare to embark on a transformative expedition toward mastering cybersecurity excellence.

Chapter 1: Foundations of Cybersecurity

Learning outcomes
- **1.1 – Understand Cybersecurity**
    - Describe the concept of cybersecurity.
    - Explain the importance of cybersecurity.
    - Describe consequences and implications of inadequate cybersecurity.
- **1.2 - Understand core terminology and key aspects of cyber security.**
    - Define Core Terminologies (Technologies) used in Cybersecurity.
    - Explain the terms good actors and bad actors.
    - Distinguish typical behaviours of good actors and bad actors.
    - Explain the motivations of good actors and bad actors.
    - Identify key sectors that are most vulnerable to a cyber-attack.
    - Compare the motivations for a cyber-attack in key sectors.
    - Consider how an actor may carry out a cyber-attack.
- **1.3 - Understand security by design principles**
    - Describe the term security by design.
    - Explore the principles of security by design.
    - State the consequences of not considering cybersecurity during the design phase.
    - Evaluate the advantages and disadvantages of security by design.

1. Introduction

In the inaugural chapter, the foundations of cybersecurity are meticulously laid out, providing readers with a comprehensive understanding of key concepts and principles. The chapter begins by delving into the intertwined realms of Cybersecurity and Information Security, elucidating their distinct scopes and the shared imperative of protecting digital assets. The juxtaposition of Cybersecurity's technology-centric focus with Information Security's strategic, risk-centric approach is artfully delineated.

The core principles of the CIA triad—Confidentiality, Integrity, and Availability—are introduced as the bedrock of secure systems, elucidating how these principles collectively form a robust framework for protecting data and systems. The chapter further expounds on essential cybersecurity terminologies, ensuring readers are equipped with a nuanced vocabulary crucial for navigating the dynamic landscape of digital security.

An exploration of the evolving terminologies segues seamlessly into an examination of Cybersecurity Concepts, elucidating terminologies ranging from firewalls to threat vectors. Readers are guided through the intricacies of critical aspects such as encryption, vulnerability management, and incident response, providing a solid foundation for subsequent chapters.

Interactive activities, quizzes, and group exercises punctuate the chapter, transforming theoretical knowledge into practical understanding. From dissecting the key differences between Cybersecurity and Information Security to engaging in real-world scenarios of cyber-attacks, readers are actively involved in their learning journey.

Finally, the chapter culminates in an exploration of the profound importance of cybersecurity in our interconnected world. From the protection of sensitive data to the preservation of privacy, prevention of cyber-attacks, and the crucial role in maintaining national security, the chapter underscores the pervasive influence of cybersecurity across various facets of our lives and businesses.

In summary, Chapter 1 serves as an indispensable primer, equipping readers with the foundational knowledge and vocabulary essential for navigating the intricate landscape of cybersecurity. The interplay of theoretical insights, practical exercises, and real-world implications lays a robust groundwork for the chapters that follow.

1.1 Concept of Cybersecurity

In the realm of digital fortification, the tandem of Cybersecurity and Information Security emerges as the vanguard against the myriad threats looming in the digital landscape. While both disciplines share the overarching goal of shielding digital assets and data, they diverge in their scopes and perspectives, each playing a unique role in the defence of our digital realm.

In essence, while Cybersecurity and Information Security share the common objective of safeguarding the digital realm, their nuances in scope, strategic orientation, and operational focus make them indispensable counterparts in the ongoing battle against the ever-evolving landscape of cyber threats.

1.1.1 Key Principles of Security - Similarities

Cybersecurity

At its core, Cybersecurity is a sentinel, staunchly guarding computer systems, networks, and the digital infrastructure that underpins our connected world. This discipline is intricately woven into the fabric of technology, focusing on operational measures to thwart cyber threats. Key concerns include preventing unauthorised access, combating cyber-attacks, and mitigating potential damages.

The spectrum of cyber threats encompasses a diverse array, including the notorious realms of hacking, malware, ransomware, and phishing. To counteract these digital assailants, cybersecurity employs a suite of measures such as firewalls, intrusion detection systems, encryption, and well-defined incident response procedures. Its modus operandi is distinctly technology-centric, as it grapples with the dynamic landscape of digital warfare.

Information Security

In a broader context, Information Security stands as the custodian of all forms of sensitive and confidential information. This discipline extends its protective mantle beyond the realms of digital bits and bytes, encapsulating physical records, intellectual property, and the vital human resources that drive the information ecosystem.

Taking a holistic and risk-centric approach, Information Security oversees the entire information lifecycle, from its inception to eventual disposal. Its strategic focus involves identifying risks, implementing robust access controls, formulating comprehensive policies, and ensuring unwavering compliance with established standards. Information Security is not merely a safeguard; it integrates seamlessly with business processes, ensuring that security becomes an inherent part of the organisational DNA.

1.1.2 Key Differences

In the intricate tapestry of digital defence, the distinctions between Cybersecurity and Information Security become pronounced, each playing a pivotal role in safeguarding our digital terrain. These disparities, ranging from scope to strategic orientation, underscore the complementary nature of these two indispensable disciplines.

Scope

At its fundamental level, the scope of Cybersecurity is sharply focused on the protection of digital assets. It stands as the digital sentinel guarding the gates of computer systems, networks, and the broader digital infrastructure. In contrast, Information Security casts a broader net, encompassing all types of sensitive information. From digital data to physical records and intellectual property, Information Security serves as the custodian of the entire information spectrum.

Focus

In the realm of threats and vulnerabilities, Cybersecurity directs its attention to specific cyber threats. Its mandate includes countering unauthorised access, thwarting cyber-attacks, and mitigating damages inflicted by hacking, malware, ransomware, and phishing. Information Security, on the other hand, adopts a panoramic view, considering the overall protection of information assets. Its concerns extend beyond specific cyber threats to the holistic well-being of the information ecosystem.

Technology-centric vs. Risk-centric

The approaches adopted by Cybersecurity and Information Security diverge in their strategic underpinnings. Cybersecurity, being more technology-centric, places a premium on technical controls. Firewalls, intrusion detection systems, encryption, and incident response procedures constitute the arsenal wielded in the digital battleground. In contrast, Information Security embraces a broader, risk-centric approach. It entails identifying risks, implementing robust access controls, formulating comprehensive policies, and ensuring compliance with established standards. Information Security's focus transcends technology to encompass a holistic risk management perspective.

Operational vs. Strategic

Cybersecurity operates as the operational bastion in the defence against cyber threats. Its modus operandi involves the day-to-day activities aimed at securing digital assets and responding to emerging threats. Conversely, Information Security assumes a strategic role, aligning its efforts with broader business objectives. It integrates seamlessly with organisational processes, ensuring that security becomes an intrinsic component of the business strategy. While Cybersecurity addresses the immediate and specific, Information Security orchestrates a strategic symphony that resonates with the overarching goals of the organisation.

In essence, the symbiotic relationship between Cybersecurity and Information Security becomes more apparent when these key differences are illuminated. Together, they form a formidable defence against the ever-evolving landscape of cyber threats, weaving a comprehensive shield that protects the digital domain from all angles.

1.1.3 Confidentiality, Integrity, Availability (CIA) Triad

In the realm of information security, the CIA Triad—Confidentiality, Integrity, and Availability—stands as a cornerstone, offering a robust framework that organisations worldwide leverage to fortify their digital fortresses. Commonly defined and embraced by leading organisations such as (ISC)², ISACA, and ISO17799, the CIA Triad encapsulates principles that are integral to protecting assets, mitigating risks, and safeguarding sensitive information.

Confidentiality

The first pillar, Confidentiality, serves as a guardian against the intentional or unintentional disclosure of sensitive data. Its mandate is to restrict access to information solely to authorised individuals or entities possessing a legitimate need. Encryption, stringent access controls, user authentication mechanisms, and the establishment of secure communication channels are the tools of the trade in upholding confidentiality. By meticulously controlling data access, this principle ensures that valuable information remains shielded from prying eyes.

Integrity

The second tenet, Integrity, is the stalwart defender of the accuracy, consistency, and trustworthiness of information across its entire lifecycle. It is designed to thwart any attempts at unauthorised modification, deletion, or corruption of data. To maintain data integrity, a suite of measures is employed, including data validation processes, checksums, digital signatures, and robust backup strategies. By implementing these measures, organisations bolster the reliability and trustworthiness of their information assets.

Availability

The third cornerstone, Availability, places a premium on ensuring the accessibility and usability of information and resources precisely when needed. It guarantees that authorised users can seamlessly access data and systems without delay. In the pursuit of availability, organisations deploy strategies such as redundancy, fault tolerance mechanisms, meticulous disaster recovery planning, real-time system monitoring, and responsive incident management mechanisms. This ensures that critical resources remain available, even in the face of unforeseen challenges.

Together, these three principles form the bedrock of a comprehensive security framework, guiding the design and implementation of secure systems. The CIA Triad not only serves as a touchstone for organisations in their quest for robust cybersecurity but also embodies a universal standard embraced by the broader information security community. As organisations navigate the dynamic digital landscape, the CIA Triad remains a steadfast guide, providing a resilient foundation for the protection of sensitive information and the preservation of the integrity and availability of digital assets.

1.1.4 Cybersecurity Terminologies

In the vast domain of cybersecurity, a diverse array of terms sheds light on the vocabulary and essential concepts necessary for comprehending and manoeuvring through this constantly changing field. This compilation offers insight into the complex lexicon of cybersecurity, enabling both individuals and organisations to navigate its intricacies. Presented below are some frequently used cybersecurity terms:

Firewall

Definition: A network security device that monitors and controls incoming and outgoing network traffic based on predefined security rules.

Purpose: To protect against unauthorised access and malicious activities by acting as a barrier between internal and external networks.

Antivirus

Definition: Software designed to detect, prevent, and remove malicious software (viruses, worms, etc.) from computer systems.

Purpose: To safeguard computer systems from malware infections and maintain the integrity of data and software.

Phishing

Definition: A fraudulent technique involving impersonation of a trustworthy entity to deceive individuals into compromising their security.

Purpose: To trick individuals into disclosing sensitive information such as login credentials, financial data, or personal details.

Social Engineering

Definition: The use of psychological manipulation to trick individuals into divulging confidential information or performing actions leading to security breaches.

Purpose: To exploit human vulnerabilities and bypass technical security measures by influencing people's behaviour.

Zero-day Vulnerability

Definition: A security vulnerability in software or systems unknown to the vendor, posing a high risk due to potential exploitation before discovery and patching.

Purpose: To highlight the urgency of timely patches and proactive security measures to mitigate the risk of exploitation.

Incident Response

Definition: The organised approach to handling and responding to security incidents, including detection, investigation, containment, and recovery.

Purpose: To minimise the impact of security breaches and restore normal operations while preserving evidence for analysis and prevention.

Data Breach

Definition: The unauthorised access, acquisition, or disclosure of sensitive or confidential data, often resulting in potential harm to individuals or organisations.

Purpose: To emphasize the importance of protecting data assets and implementing measures to prevent data breaches.

Security Policy

Definition: A documented set of rules, guidelines, and procedures defining how an organisation manages and protects its information assets and technology infrastructure.

Purpose: To establish clear expectations and standards for security practices, compliance, and risk management within an organisation.

Malware

Definition: Short for "malicious software," designed to cause harm, damage, or exploit vulnerabilities in computer systems or networks.

Purpose: To disrupt operations, steal sensitive information, or gain unauthorised access to systems for malicious purposes.

Encryption

Definition: The process of converting information into a coded format to prevent unauthorised access.

Purpose: To ensure confidentiality, integrity, and authenticity of data by encoding it in a way that only authorized parties can decipher.

Vulnerability

Definition: A weakness or flaw in a system, network, or application that can be exploited by attackers.

Purpose: To identify areas of potential risk and prioritise remediation efforts to protect against exploitation and compromise.

Patch

Definition: A software update or fix released by vendors to address identified security vulnerabilities.

Purpose: To close security gaps and strengthen defences against known threats and vulnerabilities.

Two-Factor Authentication (2FA)

Definition: A security measure requiring users to provide two different types of authentication factors to verify their identity.

Purpose: To add an extra layer of security beyond passwords and enhance identity verification for accessing sensitive resources.

Intrusion Detection System (IDS)

Definition: A security tool that monitors network traffic and system activities to identify and respond to potential security breaches.

Purpose: To detect suspicious or malicious activities, alert security teams, and mitigate threats to network infrastructure.

Penetration Testing

Definition: A method of assessing the security of a system or network by simulating real-world attacks.

Purpose: To identify vulnerabilities, weaknesses, and misconfigurations that could be exploited by attackers and recommend security enhancements.

Data Loss Prevention (DLP)

Definition: A set of technologies and practices aimed at preventing the unauthorized loss, leakage, or theft of sensitive data.

Purpose: To safeguard sensitive information from accidental or intentional disclosure, misuse, or unauthorised access.

Multi-factor Authentication (MFA)

Definition: Like 2FA, MFA requires users to provide multiple forms of authentication to verify their identity.

Purpose: To strengthen access controls and reduce the risk of unauthorised access by requiring additional authentication factors.

Security Incident

Definition: An event indicating a possible security breach, such as unauthorised access, malware infection, or data leakage.

Purpose: To prompt immediate investigation, containment, and remediation efforts to minimise the impact and prevent further harm.

Network Segmentation

Definition: The practice of dividing a computer network into smaller, isolated segments to enhance security.

Purpose: To contain the spread of threats, limit access to sensitive resources, and minimise the impact of security incidents.

Access Control

Definition: The process of managing and enforcing restrictions on user access to systems, networks, or data.

Purpose: To ensure that only authorised users have appropriate permissions to access and modify resources, reducing the risk of unauthorised activities.

Security Information and Event Management (SIEM)

Definition: A technology combining security event management and security information management to collect, analyse, and correlate security logs.

Purpose: To provide real-time visibility into security events, detect suspicious activities, and facilitate incident response and forensic analysis.

Threat Intelligence

Definition: Information about current and emerging threats that helps organisations proactively defend against cyber threats.

Purpose: To enhance threat detection, risk assessment, and decision-making by providing insights into evolving threat landscapes and adversary tactics.

Incident Response Plan (IRP)

Definition: A predefined set of procedures guiding an organisation's response to a security incident.

Purpose: To ensure a coordinated, timely, and effective response to security incidents, minimising disruption and mitigating potential damage.

Encryption Key

Definition: A piece of information used in encryption algorithms to encrypt and decrypt data.

Purpose: To protect the confidentiality and integrity of encrypted data by controlling access to cryptographic operations and ensuring secure communication channels.

Data Breach Notification

Definition: The process of notifying affected individuals, customers, or authorities in the event of a data breach.

Purpose: To fulfil legal and regulatory requirements, maintain transparency, and mitigate potential harm to affected parties.

Security Awareness Training

Definition: Programs educating individuals about common cyber threats, best practices, and security policies.

Purpose: To empower employees and stakeholders with the knowledge and skills to recognise, report, and mitigate security risks and incidents.

Threat Vector

Definition: The path or method through which a cyber threat gains access to a system or network.

Purpose: To understand and analyse potential attack paths and entry points, enabling proactive defence and risk mitigation strategies.

Incident Management

Definition: The process of managing and coordinating the response to a security incident.

Purpose: To restore normal operations, contain the impact of security breaches, and prevent recurrence through systematic incident handling and resolution.

1.1.5 What is Cybersecurity?

Security - A Fundamental Concept

At its core, security embodies the fundamental human instinct to be safe and shielded from potential threats and adversaries. It encompasses the assurance that one's well-being and possessions are safeguarded against harm or compromise.

Cyber Security

In the digital era, this concept extends into the virtual realm, giving rise to the field of cybersecurity. Have you ever come across the term? If so, what do you think it means?

Definition of Cyber Security

Spelt Cyber security or Cybersecurity, it can be defined as the practice of safeguarding computers, servers, mobile devices, electronic systems, networks, and data from a spectrum of digital threats, ranging from cyber-attacks to theft and damage. In essence, it's the digital shield that stands guard over our interconnected world.

1.1.6 The Vital Role of Cybersecurity

This practice is not merely a technological safeguard; it's a necessity for individuals, businesses, and organisations that traverse the vast landscapes of the internet for communication, accessing information, or conducting transactions. Cybersecurity is the gatekeeper that ensures the integrity and security of our digital interactions.

Applications of Cybersecurity

In our daily lives and business endeavours, cybersecurity plays a pivotal role. Some common facets where cybersecurity application is indispensable includes:

1. **Online Banking:**

    - *Definition:* The secure management and protection of financial transactions conducted over the internet.
    - *Cybersecurity Role:* Safeguarding sensitive financial data, ensuring secure transactions, and preventing unauthorised access to accounts.

2. **E-commerce:**

    - *Definition:* The buying and selling of goods and services online.
    - *Cybersecurity Role:* Protecting customer data, securing payment transactions, and ensuring the integrity of online shopping platforms.

3. **Social Media:**
    - *Definition:* Online platforms facilitating social interactions, content sharing, and networking.
    - *Cybersecurity Role:* Safeguarding user accounts, protecting personal information, and mitigating risks associated with social engineering attacks.

4. **Email Communication:**
    - *Definition:* Electronic exchange of messages and information.
    - *Cybersecurity Role:* Preventing email phishing attacks, securing communication channels, and safeguarding sensitive information exchanged via emails.

1.1.7 Types of Cyber Threats

In the dynamic landscape of cyberspace, the potential for intentional harm or interference with computer networks and systems is ever-present. It's crucial to note that cyber threats are dynamic, constantly evolving, and new types continue to emerge. To mitigate risks, organisations and individuals must stay informed, implement robust cybersecurity practices, and regularly update their systems. Staying vigilant and adapting to emerging threats is key to maintaining a resilient defence against the ever-changing landscape of cyber threats.

The following are common types of cyber threats that individuals and organisations should be vigilant against:

1. **Malware:**
    - *Description:* Malicious software encompassing viruses, worms, Trojans, ransomware, and spyware, capable of damaging or disrupting computer systems.

2. **Phishing:**
    - *Description:* Attempts to trick users into revealing sensitive information through deceptive emails, messages, or websites, disguised as trustworthy entities.

3. **Denial of Service (DoS) and Distributed Denial of Service (DDoS) Attacks:**
    - *Description:* Overwhelming a system or network with excessive traffic, rendering it unavailable to legitimate users.

4. **Social Engineering:**
   - *Description:* Manipulating individuals to gain unauthorised access or divulge sensitive information through psychological manipulation and deception.

5. **Man-in-the-Middle (MitM) Attacks:**
   - *Description:* Intercepting and altering communication between two parties without their knowledge, allowing eavesdropping or data manipulation.

6. **SQL Injection:**
   - *Description:* Exploiting vulnerabilities to inject malicious SQL code, enabling unauthorised access to databases and potential data theft.

7. **Zero-day Exploits:**
   - *Description:* Exploiting unknown software vulnerabilities before discovery or patching, gaining unauthorised access.

8. **Ransomware:**
   - *Description:* Encrypting files on a victim's system, demanding a ransom payment in exchange for restoring access to encrypted data.

9. **Insider Threats:**
   - *Description:* Malicious activities conducted by individuals within an organisation, exploiting authorised access to cause harm.

10. **Advanced Persistent Threats (APTs):**
    - *Description:* Targeted and prolonged attacks by skilled adversaries seeking unauthorised access for espionage or financial gain.

11. **Password Attacks:**
    - *Description:* Attempts to gain unauthorised access by cracking or guessing passwords using techniques like brute force or dictionary attacks.

12. **Malicious Insiders:**
    - *Description:* Trusted individuals within an organisation abusing privileges for unauthorised activities such as data theft or sabotage.

13. **Advanced Malware:**

- *Description:* Sophisticated malware designed to bypass traditional security measures and carry out specific malicious activities.

14. **Botnets:**

    - *Description:* Networks of compromised computers, controlled for malicious activities like DDoS attacks, spam distribution, or data theft.

15. **Cryptojacking:**

    - *Description:* Illegitimate use of computing resources to mine cryptocurrencies without knowledge or consent, causing system slowdowns.

16. **Wi-Fi Eavesdropping:**

    - *Description:* Unauthorised interception of Wi-Fi communications to capture sensitive information transmitted over wireless networks.

17. **Eavesdropping and Surveillance:**

    - *Description:* Unauthorised monitoring or interception of communications, including phone calls, emails, or instant messages.

18. **Web Application Attacks:**

    - *Description:* Exploiting vulnerabilities in web applications to gain unauthorised access, manipulate data, or deface websites.

19. **Supply Chain Attacks:**

    - *Description:* Targeting vulnerabilities in the supply chain to compromise trusted software or hardware components for unauthorised access or malware distribution.

20. **Internet of Things (IoT) Vulnerabilities:**

    - *Description:* Exploiting security weaknesses in internet-connected devices to gain control or access sensitive data.

1.1.8 Cyber Attack Response Plans

Group Activity 1

In pairs or in groups of 3:

Each group has a scenario involving a cyber-attack to which you must produce a plan to prevent or respond to the attack.
- **Scenario 1;** a phishing email that asks for personal information.
- **Scenario 2;** a virus that infects a computer.
- **Scenario 3;** a ransomware attack that locks down a company's data.

After developing the plans, each group can present their strategies on say, a Padlet Wall, fostering collaborative learning and sharing insights within the class.

Possible Solutions

Scenario 1: Phishing Email Requesting Personal Information

Prevention Plan:
1. **Employee Training:** Conduct regular phishing awareness training sessions for all employees to educate them on identifying and reporting phishing attempts.
2. **Email Filtering:** Implement advanced email filtering solutions to automatically detect and quarantine suspicious emails before they reach employees.
3. **Multi-Factor Authentication (MFA):** Enforce MFA for accessing sensitive systems and accounts to add an extra layer of security even if credentials are compromised.
4. **Security Policies:** Develop and communicate clear policies regarding the sharing of personal information via email, emphasizing that such requests should be verified through other means.

Response Plan:
1. **Reporting Mechanism:** Establish a clear process for employees to report phishing emails promptly.
2. **Isolation:** Isolate affected systems to prevent further compromise.
3. **Investigation:** Conduct a thorough investigation to identify the extent of the phishing attack and any compromised information.
4. **Communication:** Notify relevant stakeholders about the incident, providing guidance on potential impacts and necessary actions.

5. **Incident Documentation:** Document all actions taken during the incident response for future analysis and improvement.

Scenario 2: Computer Infected by a Virus

Prevention Plan:
1. **Antivirus Software:** Ensure that all computers have up-to-date antivirus software installed and regularly conduct scans.
2. **Employee Training:** Educate employees on safe browsing habits and the dangers of downloading files from untrusted sources.
3. **Patch Management:** Implement a robust patch management system to ensure that operating systems and software are updated regularly.
4. **Network Segmentation:** Divide the network into segments to contain the spread of a potential infection.

Response Plan:
1. **Isolation:** Immediately disconnect the infected computer from the network to prevent the virus from spreading.
2. **Antivirus Scan:** Run a thorough antivirus scan on the infected computer to identify and remove the malicious software.
3. **System Restore:** If possible, restore the affected system to a previous clean state using system backup or restore points.
4. **User Notification:** Notify the user of the infected system about the incident and provide guidance on secure computing practices.
5. **Incident Documentation:** Document all actions taken during the incident response for analysis and improvement.

Scenario 3: Ransomware Attack Locking Down Company's Data

Prevention Plan:
1. **Regular Backups:** Perform regular backups of critical data and ensure their integrity. Store backups in an isolated environment.
2. **Security Awareness Training:** Train employees to recognise and avoid clicking on suspicious links or downloading attachments from unknown sources.
3. **Network Segmentation:** Implement network segmentation to limit the lateral movement of ransomware within the network.

4. **Email Filtering:** Strengthen email filtering to detect and block ransomware-laden emails.

Response Plan:
1. **Isolation:** Isolate infected systems and disconnect them from the network to prevent further encryption.

2. **Identify Ransomware Variant:** Determine the specific ransomware variant to explore potential decryption solutions.

3. **Restore from Backups:** Restore affected systems and data from backups, ensuring the restoration of clean and uninfected data.

4. **Law Enforcement Notification:** Report the incident to law enforcement authorities.

5. **User Communication:** Communicate with affected users, providing guidance on security measures and reinforcing the importance of reporting suspicious activities.

6. **Incident Documentation:** Document all response actions, detailing lessons learned for future improvements.

Tutorial Activity 2 - Cybersecurity Quiz
1. What is the term used to describe a type of cyber-attack where an attacker uses multiple compromised devices to flood a network or website with traffic, making it inaccessible to legitimate users?

    - Phishing
    - Ransomware
    - DDoS attack
    - Malware

2. Which of the following is an example of a strong password?

    - Password123
    - 123456
    - G0ldf1sh!2$
    - qwerty

1.1.9 Importance of Cybersecurity

In the contemporary landscape, the internet has seamlessly woven itself into the fabric of our lives, offering unparalleled access to information, entertainment, and communication. However, this digital interconnectedness also ushers in the omnipresent spectre of cyber threats - malware, phishing, ransomware, and cyberattacks - that lurk in the virtual shadows.

Risks Associated with Cyber Threats

The convenience and accessibility the internet affords also expose individuals and organisations to significant risks. Cyber threats have the potential to inflict not only financial losses but also damage to reputation and, in extreme cases, physical harm.

Crucial Domains of Cybersecurity

Given the omnipresence of the internet and the diverse array of cyber threats, cybersecurity emerges as an imperative shield against potential harm. This significance extends beyond individual users to encompass entire organisations.

Importance in Daily Lives and Business

1. **Online Banking:**
   - *Importance:* Safeguarding financial transactions and sensitive data from unauthorised access, ensuring the integrity of online financial activities.

2. **E-commerce:**
   - *Importance:* Providing a secure environment for online buying and selling, protecting customer information, and fostering trust in digital transactions.

3. **Social Media:**
   - *Importance:* Shielding user accounts, personal information, and preventing the spread of malicious content or social engineering attacks.

4. **Email Communication:**
   - *Importance:* Ensuring the confidentiality of email exchanges, protecting against phishing attempts, and securing sensitive information.

Global Impact

The importance of cybersecurity transcends individual experiences, influencing the global landscape of digital interactions. The interconnectedness of the modern world means that a cyber threat in one corner of the globe can reverberate globally, underscoring the collective responsibility to fortify digital defences.

Financial Losses and Reputation Management

For businesses, the repercussions of a cyber-attack extend beyond immediate financial losses. The erosion of trust and damage to reputation can have enduring consequences, making cybersecurity a linchpin for sustainable business practices.

Personal Well-being and Privacy

On an individual level, cybersecurity safeguards personal well-being, ensuring the privacy and security of sensitive information. This protection becomes increasingly vital as digital interactions become more intertwined with our daily lives.

Categories and Significance of Cybersecurity

In the digital age, the growing significance of cybersecurity is underscored by its multifaceted contributions to various aspects of our interconnected world. The multifaceted importance of cybersecurity radiates across the protection of sensitive data, preservation of privacy, prevention of cyber-attacks, continuity of operations, protection of national security, trust and reputation, and legal and regulatory compliance. In an era defined by digital connectivity, the robustness of cybersecurity measures becomes integral to fostering a secure and resilient digital landscape. Let's categorise and explore these crucial dimensions:

1. **Protection of Sensitive Data:**
   - *Explanation:* Cybersecurity is essential for safeguarding sensitive data, including personal information, financial details, and intellectual property, from unauthorized access, theft, and damage.

2. **Preservation of Privacy:**
   - *Explanation:* It preserves privacy by thwarting unauthorized surveillance, preventing data mining, and ensuring the confidentiality of personal information, thereby maintaining the privacy of individuals' online activities.

3. **Prevention of Cyber Attacks:**
   - *Explanation:* Cybersecurity measures are crucial in preventing a spectrum of cyber-attacks, including malware, ransomware, phishing, and hacking. These measures mitigate the risks of financial losses, service disruptions, and reputational damage.

4. **Continuity of Operations:**
   - *Explanation:* Cybersecurity ensures the continuity of operations by safeguarding critical infrastructure, minimizing downtime, and reducing the risk of costly recovery efforts in the aftermath of cyber incidents.

5. **Protection of National Security:**
   - *Explanation:* Cybersecurity plays a pivotal role in national security by defending against cyber espionage, protecting governmental institutions, defence systems, and critical infrastructure from cyber threats.

6. **Trust and Reputation:**
   - *Explanation:* Building trust and maintaining a positive reputation are bolstered through cybersecurity. Assurance of secure data promotes trust among customers and users, facilitating engagement and secure online transactions.

7. **Legal and Regulatory Compliance:**
   - *Explanation:* Robust cybersecurity practices ensure compliance with legal and regulatory requirements. Adhering to these standards helps organizations avoid legal consequences, financial penalties, and reputational damage.

1.1.10 Consequences and Implications of Inadequate Cybersecurity

Tutorial Activity 3

- ***Question:*** *What are the consequences and implications of insufficient cybersecurity that you are aware of?*
- ***Instructions:***
    - Individually or in Pairs, state as many as you know (or can think of) giving examples where possible.
    - Then **Snowball** into groups of 4 then compare and contrast your answers making corrections where necessary.

- o   Showcase group findings to the class.

Individual or Pair Brainstorming:
1. **Data Breaches and Loss of Sensitive Information:**
    - *Example:* Exposure of personal details in a healthcare data breach leading to identity theft.

2. **Financial Losses:**
    - *Example:* Costs associated with remediation, legal proceedings, and regulatory fines after a successful cyber-attack.

3. **Business Disruption and Downtime:**
    - *Example:* Extended downtime due to a ransomware attack, causing operational disruptions and financial losses.

4. **Damage to Reputation and Trust:**
    - *Example:* Negative publicity and customer distrust following the disclosure of a data breach.

5. **Legal and Regulatory Consequences:**
    - *Example:* Fines and legal liabilities for non-compliance with data protection regulations.

6. **Intellectual Property Theft:**
    - *Example:* Unauthorised access to and theft of proprietary software source code.

7. **Loss of Competitive Advantage:**
    - *Example:* Competitors gaining access to strategic business plans through a cybersecurity breach.

8. **Disruption of Critical Infrastructure:**
    - *Example:* Cyber-attack on a power grid leading to widespread power outages.

9. **Increased Cybercrime and Cyber Threats:**
   - *Example:* Proliferation of phishing attacks targeting individuals with weak cybersecurity measures.

10. **Insider Threats and Employee Morale:**
    - *Example:* An employee intentionally leaking sensitive company information.

11. **Geopolitical and National Security Implications:**
    - *Example:* Cyber-attack on government institutions leading to compromised national security.

Group Comparison and Contrast

In groups of four, participants can share their individual or paired answers, identifying commonalities, differences, and potential additions. Discussions can include examples, real-world scenarios, and insights into the overarching themes of each consequence.

Showcasing Group Findings

Each group can present their consolidated findings to the class, providing a comprehensive overview of the consequences and implications of inadequate cybersecurity. The discussion can include a focus on preventive measures and the collective responsibility of individuals and organisations to bolster cybersecurity practices.

Tutorial Activity 4

Quiz: Consequences and Implications of Inadequate Cybersecurity

1. What is one of the potential consequences of inadequate cybersecurity?
   a) Data breaches and theft of sensitive information
   b) Improved customer trust and loyalty
   c) Enhanced reputation in the market
   d) Increased efficiency in business operations

2. Which of the following is an implication of inadequate cybersecurity for individuals?
   a) Financial loss due to stolen credit card information
   b) Improved personal privacy and data protection.
   c) Increased productivity in personal tasks

d) Enhanced online shopping experience.

3. Inadequate cybersecurity can lead to which of the following for organisations?

    a) Damage to brand reputation and customer trust.

    b) Better compliance with data protection regulations

    c) Reduced operational costs.

    d) Higher employee morale and job satisfaction

4. What is one of the potential consequences of inadequate cybersecurity?

    a) Increased resilience against cyber threats
    b) Compliance with industry standards and regulations
    c) Loss of intellectual property and trade secrets
    d) Streamlined communication and collaboration within teams.

5. Which of the following is an implication of inadequate cybersecurity for governments?

    a) Strengthening national security and defence

    b) Protection of critical infrastructure from cyberattacks.

    c) Vulnerability to cyber espionage and attacks on sensitive data

    d) Economic growth and development

6. Inadequate cybersecurity can lead to which of the following for individuals?

    a) Identity theft and unauthorized access to personal accounts

    b) Improved accessibility to online services

    c) Enhanced control over personal information shared online.

    d) Increased personal safety in the digital realm.

7. **What is one of the potential consequences of inadequate cybersecurity?**

    a) Improved system performance and efficiency

    b) Protection against phishing attacks and scams

    c) Disruption of critical services and infrastructure

    d) Facilitation of seamless digital transformation

8. Which of the following is an implication of inadequate cybersecurity for small businesses?

    a) Enhanced competitiveness and market share

    b) Loss of customer trust and loyalty

    c) Access to innovative technologies and tools

    d) Expansion of business operations globally

9. Inadequate cybersecurity can lead to which of the following for society?

    a) Strengthening social connections and relationships

    b) Protection of personal data from unauthorized access

    c) Increased vulnerability to cybercrimes and frauds

    d) Improved access to quality education and healthcare

1.2 Understand Core Terminology and Key Aspects of Cybersecurity

In the ever-evolving landscape of cybersecurity, a foundational grasp of core terminology and key technological aspects is imperative. Below, we delve into the essential concepts that form the backbone of this critical field.

1.2.1 Define Core Terminologies (Technologies) Used in Cybersecurity

- **Cloud**

    In the realm of cybersecurity, the cloud refers to the practice of storing, processing, and managing data and applications on remote servers that are accessed over the internet. This paradigm shift in data handling has both expanded capabilities and introduced novel security considerations.

- **Domain**

    A domain is a discrete group of devices or resources within a network, all subject to a common administrative authority and identified by a unique name. Understanding domains is fundamental in delineating network boundaries and establishing access controls.

- **BYOD (Bring Your Own Device)**

    This policy allows employees to utilize their personal devices for work-related tasks. While fostering flexibility and efficiency, it introduces a spectrum of security risks that necessitate robust mitigation strategies. Striking a balance between convenience and security is paramount.

- **Web Application Firewalls (WAF)**

    These pivotal security tools serve as sentinels guarding web applications against an array of attacks. WAFs operate by vigilantly monitoring and filtering network traffic, acting as a crucial defence against threats that target vulnerabilities in web applications.

- **AI (Artificial Intelligence) and ML (Machine Learning)**

    These transformative techniques emulate human intelligence and empower machines to learn from data. In the realm of cybersecurity, they play a pivotal role in threat detection and decision-making. The dynamic nature of cyber threats demands adaptive, intelligent systems capable of discerning evolving patterns.

- **SSL/TLS (Secure Sockets Layer/Transport Layer Security)**

    These cryptographic protocols form the bedrock of secure online communication. They establish an encrypted connection between a web server and a client, ensuring that sensitive data traverses the internet in a secure and confidential manner. SSL/TLS protocols are instrumental in safeguarding against eavesdropping and data tampering.

Acquiring proficiency in these core terminologies lays the foundation for a robust comprehension of cybersecurity principles. As we navigate the intricate landscapes of data protection and threat mitigation, a firm grasp of these concepts becomes indispensable.

1.2.2 Explain the Terms Good Actors and Bad Actors

In the realm of cybersecurity, the distinction between "good actors" and "bad actors" is paramount in understanding the motivations and actions of individuals or entities within the digital landscape.

- **Good Actors**

    These are individuals, organizations, or entities that operate within the bounds of legal and ethical frameworks. They prioritize security, integrity, and confidentiality of data. Good actors often include security professionals, ethical hackers, and law-abiding citizens who work towards safeguarding digital environments.

- **Bad Actors**

    Conversely, bad actors are individuals, groups, or entities that engage in activities that breach legal and ethical boundaries. Their actions are typically driven by malicious intent, seeking to exploit vulnerabilities, steal sensitive information, or disrupt digital operations. Bad actors encompass cybercriminals, hackers with malicious intent, and entities engaged in cyber espionage or warfare.

Understanding the motivations and tactics of both good and bad actors is crucial in developing effective cybersecurity strategies. It allows for the identification of potential threats and the implementation of measures to mitigate risks.

1.2.3 Distinguish Typical Behaviours of Good Actors and Bad Actors

Recognising the distinctive behaviours of Good Actors and Bad Actors enables cybersecurity professionals to effectively assess and respond to potential threats. It forms the bedrock for developing strategies that safeguard digital assets and networks from the actions of bad actors, while upholding the principles of ethical and lawful conduct.

1.2.3.1 Behaviours of Good Actors

1. **Adherence to Legal and Ethical Standards**: Good actors operate within the confines of established legal and ethical frameworks, respecting privacy rights and intellectual property.

2. **Proactive Security Measures**: They prioritize proactive measures to protect systems and data, such as implementing strong access controls, encryption, and regular security audits.

3. **Collaborative Efforts**: Good actors often engage in information sharing and collaboration with the broader cybersecurity community to enhance collective defence against emerging threats.

4. **Continuous Learning and Skill Development**: They invest in staying updated with the latest security technologies, trends, and best practices, contributing to the overall advancement of cybersecurity.

Behaviours of Bad Actors

1. **Exploitation of Vulnerabilities:** Bad actors seek out vulnerabilities in systems, applications, or networks with the intent of exploiting them for personal gain or to cause harm.

2. **Malicious Intent:** Their actions are driven by malicious intent, which may include stealing sensitive data, conducting financial fraud, or disrupting critical operations.

3. **Evasion and Deception:** Bad actors often employ techniques to evade detection, such as using anonymising tools or employing advanced evasion tactics to bypass security measures.

4. **Lack of Ethical Considerations:** They disregard legal and ethical boundaries, often engaging in activities that compromise privacy, integrity, and confidentiality of data.

1.2.4 Grey Hat Hackers: Bridging the Divide

Within the dynamic landscape of cybersecurity, a distinctive category exists, operating in a morally ambiguous territory - the "Grey Hat" hacker. Their actions straddle the line between ethical and potentially unlawful, presenting a unique paradigm in the cybersecurity community.

A ***Grey Hat Hacker*** is an individual who operates with intentions that transcend the traditional labels of "good" or "bad" actors. Unlike black hat hackers, who typically engage in malicious activities, or white hat hackers, who work within legal and ethical boundaries, grey hat hackers navigate a middle ground.

Motivation and Intentions

Grey hat hackers are motivated by a genuine desire to bolster security measures rather than inflict harm. They might undertake actions that could be deemed unauthorized or even bordering on the cusp of illegality. Their primary objective is to expose vulnerabilities in systems, applications, or networks, often without formal permission.

Raising Awareness and Strengthening Security

One of the defining characteristics of grey hat hackers is their aim to raise awareness and assist organisations in fortifying their security posture. By unveiling vulnerabilities, they provide valuable insights that organisations can use to fortify their defences.

Ethics and Intent

While their actions may be ethically questionable due to the potentially unauthorised nature of their activities, grey hat hackers do not harbour malicious intent. Their end goal is to catalyse improvements in security, rather than exploit weaknesses for personal gain or to cause harm.

Community Emphasis on Ethical Boundaries

It's crucial to note that the term "grey hat hacker" lacks a universally agreed-upon definition within the cybersecurity community. As such, ethical and legal boundaries are highly emphasized. Responsible security testing and disclosure practices are encouraged to ensure that the actions of grey hat hackers remain constructive and aligned with the greater objective of enhancing cybersecurity.

Understanding the role of grey hat hackers is essential in appreciating the nuanced landscape of cybersecurity. Their distinctive approach serves as a reminder that the motives behind cybersecurity activities are as varied and multifaceted as the digital landscape itself.

1.2.5 Types of Threat Actors: Understanding Motivations and Objectives

In the intricate realm of cybersecurity, it is essential to recognise the diverse array of threat actors, each driven by distinct motivations and objectives. By comprehending their intents, we can better fortify our defences against potential attacks.

- **Cybercriminals**

    Description: Cybercriminals are akin to black hat hackers, often operating as either independent agents or within large, organized cybercrime syndicates. Their primary focus revolves around illicit financial gains.

    Goal: The principal aim of cybercriminals is to amass financial or personal gain through various means of cyber exploitation. Their tactics can range from stealing sensitive information for resale to conducting financial fraud.

- **Script Kiddies**

    Description: Script Kiddies represent a group of relatively inexperienced threat actors who lack the technical acumen of advanced hackers. Instead, they rely on pre-existing scripts, tools, and exploits to cause disruption, often without a clear profit motive.

    Goal: Unlike cybercriminals, Script Kiddies are primarily motivated by a desire for recognition or notoriety. Their actions are more geared towards creating disturbances rather than pursuing a strictly destructive agenda. Nonetheless, their activities can lead to costly security incidents.

- **Hacktivists**

    Description: Hacktivists are a distinct category of threat actors driven by political, philosophical, or religious beliefs. Their actions are geared towards promoting a specific cause or ideology.

    Goal: The primary objectives of hacktivists include exposing information, defacing websites, and executing denial-of-service attacks. Their intent is to draw attention to their cause and potentially influence public opinion or policy.

- **Inside Actors (Ex-Employees)**

    Description: Inside actors are individuals who currently or previously had authorized access to an organization's networks, systems, or data. This category encompasses current or former employees, contractors, or consultants.

    Goal: The motivations of inside actors can vary widely. They may be driven by financial gain, personal discontent, or a desire for revenge against the organization. Their actions can pose significant threats due to their intimate knowledge of the organisation's infrastructure.

Understanding the distinct profiles and motivations of threat actors is integral to devising effective cybersecurity strategies. By tailoring defences to anticipate potential threats, organisations can better safeguard their digital assets and infrastructure. Additionally, vigilance and proactive measures are crucial in maintaining robust cybersecurity in an ever-evolving threat landscape.

1.2.6 Motivations of Good and Bad Actors in Cybersecurity

In the intricate world of cybersecurity, understanding the motivations that drive both good and bad actors is fundamental to devising effective defence strategies. These motivations are multifaceted and can stem from a variety of factors, creating a dynamic landscape of cyber threats.

Good Actors in Cybersecurity

1. ***Desire for Protection and Security:*** Good actors are primarily motivated by the aspiration to safeguard digital systems, networks, and data from potential threats. They recognise the critical importance of maintaining a secure digital environment.

2. ***Sense of Responsibility:*** A profound sense of responsibility drives good actors to protect individuals, organizations, and society at large from cyber threats. They understand the collective impact of their efforts on the broader digital community.

3. ***Commitment to Ethical Standards:*** Good actors adhere steadfastly to ethical principles. They prioritize privacy, respect for individual rights, and the preservation of information integrity in their pursuit of cybersecurity.

4. ***Prevention of Cybercrime:*** Good actors work diligently to thwart cybercriminal activities. Their objective is to curtail the incidence of cybercrimes, which range from identity theft to financial fraud, thereby bolstering trust in technology.

Bad Actors in Cybersecurity
1. ***Personal Gain:*** Bad actors are often motivated by personal gain, which can manifest in various forms—be it financial, political, or driven by malicious intent. Their actions are primarily oriented towards self-benefit.

2. ***Engagement in Malicious Activities:*** Bad actors engage in a wide array of nefarious activities, including hacking, perpetrating data breaches, and conducting cyber espionage. These activities are geared towards exploiting vulnerabilities in systems and networks.

3. ***Desire to Exploit and Disrupt:*** Their motivation lies in exploiting vulnerabilities to steal sensitive information or disrupt systems for various purposes. This may involve activities ranging from financial fraud to politically motivated cyber-attacks.

4. ***Diverse Range of Actors:*** Bad actors encompass a broad spectrum, including organised criminal groups, state-sponsored entities, or individuals with malicious intent. Their motivations may be rooted in financial gain, political objectives, or a desire to sow chaos in the digital realm.

5. ***Desire to Exploit and Disrupt:*** Their motivation lies in exploiting vulnerabilities to steal sensitive information or disrupt systems for various purposes. This may involve activities ranging from financial fraud to politically motivated cyber-attacks.

6. ***Diverse Range of Actors:*** Bad actors encompass a broad spectrum, including organized criminal groups, state-sponsored entities, or individuals with malicious intent. Their motivations may be rooted in financial gain, political objectives, or a desire to sow chaos in the digital realm.

1.2.7 Key Vulnerable Sectors in Cybersecurity

In the ever-evolving landscape of cyber threats, certain sectors stand out as particularly susceptible due to the nature of the information they handle. Recognising these vulnerabilities is crucial in fortifying defences and implementing targeted cybersecurity measures.

- **Financial Institutions**

    Description: Financial institutions, including banks and credit unions, are enticing targets for cybercriminals due to the potential for substantial financial gain. They manage a treasure trove of sensitive information, including credit card details, bank account information, and other financial data.

Risk: The potential loss of financial data can lead to significant financial losses for both institutions and their customers. Identity theft and fraudulent transactions are imminent threats.

- **Healthcare and Health Science**

    Description: The healthcare sector holds a wealth of electronic health records containing personal, medical, and financial information. This sector has witnessed a surge in breaches, as medical records are lucrative targets for cybercriminals engaged in identity theft and fraud.

    Risk: Breaches in this sector can have severe consequences, including compromised patient confidentiality and potential health-related fraud.

- **Educational Institutions**

    Description: Educational institutions house a trove of valuable data, encompassing personal and financial information of students and staff. This information is highly appealing to cybercriminals, especially in cases where security measures may be less robust.

    Risk: Breaches in educational institutions can result in compromised student and staff data, potentially leading to identity theft and financial fraud.

- **Retailers**

    Description: Retailers handle vast volumes of customer payment information through various channels, including online transactions and point-of-sale systems. Cybercriminals target retailers to pilfer credit card information and other valuable data.

    Risk: Retailer breaches can result in the theft of customer financial information, leading to fraudulent transactions and financial losses for both the retailer and their customers.

- **Government**

    Description: Government agencies are entrusted with highly sensitive and classified information. This sector is a prime target for state-sponsored attacks and cyber espionage, driven by geopolitical motives and potential impacts on national security.

    Risk: Breaches in government agencies can lead to significant national security risks, compromising confidential information and potentially influencing geopolitical dynamics.

- **Manufacturing**

Description: Manufacturers are susceptible to intellectual property theft, sabotage, and operational disruption. Cyber-attacks in this sector can manipulate equipment and manufacturing processes, potentially resulting in product defects and financial losses.

Risk: Intellectual property theft can lead to a loss of competitive advantage, while equipment manipulation can result in compromised product quality and financial ramifications.

Understanding the unique vulnerabilities of these sectors allows for the development of tailored cybersecurity strategies. By implementing targeted defences and proactive measures, organisations within these sectors can better safeguard their valuable information and operations against potential cyber threats.

1.2.8 Motivations for Cyber-Attacks Across Key Sectors

In the diverse landscape of cyber threats, motivations behind cyber-attacks can differ significantly based on the targeted sector. Understanding these motivations is pivotal in developing targeted defence strategies.

- **Financial Gain**

    Description: Cyber-attacks driven by the pursuit of financial gain are prevalent across various sectors. Attackers seek to steal valuable financial data, such as credit card numbers, with the intent of profiting monetarily.

    Sectors Impacted: Financial institutions, retailers, healthcare, and manufacturing.

- **Insider Threats**

    Description: Insider threats originate from individuals with authorized access to critical information within an organization. Their motivations can range from personal gain to a desire to tarnish the organization's reputation.

    Sectors Impacted: All sectors, with a heightened risk in organizations with extensive internal access to sensitive data.

- **Recognition & Popularity**

    Description: Some hackers carry out cyber-attacks with the aim of gaining recognition or notoriety within the hacking community. Their actions may be fuelled by a desire for acknowledgment.

    Sectors Impacted: All sectors, though this motivation may be more prominent in the cyber underground.

- **State-Sponsored Hackers**

    Description: Nation-states may engage in cyber-attacks for political, military, or economic objectives. These attacks can target foreign governments, terrorist groups, and corporations, often with strategic goals in mind.

    Sectors Impacted: Government, critical infrastructure, military, and corporations with significant geopolitical influence.

- **Crackers**

    Description: Crackers are individuals who manipulate software to bypass licensing and gain unauthorised access to applications or services, often at the expense of security.

    Sectors Impacted: Primarily software development but can have ramifications in any sector utilising compromised software.

- **Hacktivists**

    Description: Hacktivists carry out cyber-attacks to further political or social ideologies. Their actions may include leaking sensitive information or orchestrating Distributed Denial of Service (DDoS) attacks to make a statement.

    Sectors Impacted: Government, corporations, organisations involved in contentious political or social issues.

Recognising these diverse motivations allows for the tailoring of cybersecurity strategies to address specific threats within each sector. A nuanced understanding of these drivers empowers organisations to fortify their defences and respond effectively to potential cyber threats.

1.2.9 The Cyber Kill Chain: Understanding the Stages of a Cyber-Attack

In the intricate nuance of cyber-attacks, threat actors follow a structured series of steps, collectively known as the Cyber Kill Chain. This framework provides invaluable insights into the methods employed by attackers to infiltrate and compromise digital environments.

1. **Reconnaissance/Survey**

    In this initial phase, attackers embark on gathering crucial intelligence about their target. This includes details about employees, system configurations, and any identified vulnerabilities.

2. **Weaponisation**

   Armed with the acquired intelligence, attackers craft malicious software or exploit code tailored to exploit the identified vulnerabilities. This weaponised payload is designed to compromise the target.

3. **Delivery**

   The weaponised payload is delivered to the target's environment. This can occur through various means, with common tactics being phishing emails or enticing links that, when clicked, initiate the download of the malware.

4. **Exploitation/Breach**

   Once the malicious code is executed within the victim's system, a breach occurs. This breach grants attackers unauthorised access to the compromised system or network.

5. **Installation**

   Attackers establish persistence within the compromised system. This involves creating backdoors or additional access points, allowing them to maintain control even after initial entry.

6. **Anti-Forensics/Command and Control**

   To avoid detection, attackers employ techniques that hinder forensic investigation. Simultaneously, they establish a command-and-control infrastructure, enabling them to remotely manage the compromised system.

7. **Action on Objective**

   With a firm grip on the compromised system, attackers proceed to execute their intended actions. This could range from exfiltrating sensitive data to launching more overt attacks like Distributed Denial of Service (DDoS) assaults.

Throughout this intricate process, attackers are driven by the objective of achieving their goals while evading detection and retaining control over the compromised systems. Understanding the Cyber Kill Chain equips cybersecurity professionals with a critical framework to develop effective countermeasures and strategies to defend against such attacks. By anticipating each stage, organisations can proactively implement safeguards to thwart potential threats and mitigate their impact.

1.3 Security by Design Principles

Security by Design is a fundamental approach to building robust and secure systems from the ground up. It involves integrating security measures into every phase of a product or system's design, development, and implementation. This proactive stance ensures that security becomes an intrinsic part of the entire lifecycle of a product or system, rather than being tacked on as an afterthought, which can lead to vulnerabilities.

1.3.1 Principles of Security by Design

With Security by Design principles, organizations can construct resilient and secure systems that are better equipped to withstand evolving cybersecurity challenges. This approach instils a proactive security mindset, making it an integral part of the system's DNA rather than a mere add-on.

- **Default Security**

    Systems should be designed with secure configurations as their default settings. This includes implementing robust authentication mechanisms and access controls from the outset, reducing the potential for security gaps.

- **Least Privilege**

    Users and systems should be granted only the minimum level of privileges necessary for their specific functions. This principle limits potential damage in the event of a breach by restricting unnecessary access.

- **Défense in Depth**

    This principle emphasizes the implementation of multiple layers of security controls. Should one layer fail or be bypassed, additional layers provide an added safeguard, ensuring that the entire system is not compromised.

- **Secure Communication**

    All communication channels should be designed with security in mind. This involves the use of encryption protocols to safeguard data in transit, preventing unauthorized access or tampering.

- **Continuous Monitoring**

    Systems should be under continuous surveillance to promptly detect and respond to security events and incidents. This proactive monitoring helps identify potential threats before they can cause significant damage.

- **Regular Updates and Patches**

Systems should be designed to facilitate the straightforward application of security updates and patches. This ensures that vulnerabilities are promptly addressed, maintaining the system's resilience against emerging threats.

- **User Awareness and Training**

    Security awareness and training programs are crucial components of a robust security framework. They educate users about best practices, potential threats, and how to respond to security incidents, empowering them to be an active part of the defence against cyber threats.

1.3.2 Consequences of Neglecting Cybersecurity in the Design Phase

Neglecting cybersecurity considerations during the design phase of a system can have serious repercussions, impacting both the organisation and its stakeholders. Potential consequences include:

- **Increased Vulnerabilities**

    Without proper security measures integrated from the beginning, systems may have inherent vulnerabilities that attackers can exploit, making them more susceptible to breaches.

- **Data Breaches and Loss**

    Inadequate security measures can lead to data breaches, resulting in the exposure of sensitive information. This can have significant privacy and financial implications for individuals and organizations.

- **Financial Loss**

    Cyberattacks can lead to substantial financial losses. Expenses may include incident response efforts, legal actions, and resources devoted to damage control and recovery.

- **Legal and Regulatory Consequences**

    Neglecting cybersecurity can lead to non-compliance with industry-specific regulations and legal mandates. This can result in legal actions, fines, and other penalties.

- **Operational Disruptions**

    Cybersecurity incidents can disrupt normal business operations and services. This can lead to lost productivity, missed opportunities, and dissatisfied customers.

- **Damage to Reputation**

    Breaches and security incidents can significantly damage an organisation's reputation. The revelation of a breach can lead to negative publicity, customer loss, and a painstaking journey of reputation repair.

- **Intellectual Property Theft**

    Inadequate security measures may expose valuable intellectual property to theft. Competitors or malicious actors may steal trade secrets, potentially compromising an organisation's competitive edge.

It is crucial for organizations to recognize the potential consequences of neglecting cybersecurity during the design phase. Proactively integrating security measures from the outset is a critical step in mitigating these risks and ensuring the long-term security and resilience of the system or product.

1.3.3 Evaluation of Security by Design

Security by Design offers significant advantages such as proactive protection, cost-effectiveness, and enhanced resilience. However, organisations must carefully balance security considerations with other factors to achieve optimal results. This may involve carefully weighing the benefits against potential complexities and resource investments, all while remaining vigilant in the face of evolving cyber threats.

Advantages of Security by Design
1. **Proactive Approach:** By identifying vulnerabilities early in the design phase, Security by Design takes a proactive stance, reducing the risk of breaches.

2. **Reduced Costs:** Implementing security measures from the outset prevents the need for costly retrofits and potential legal consequences associated with security breaches.

3. **Improved Resilience:** The incorporation of multiple layers of security enhances the overall robustness and resilience of the system against potential threats.

4. **Enhanced Privacy and Compliance:** Security by Design aligns with data protection regulations, ensuring that privacy considerations are integrated into the system's design.

5. **User-Friendly Security:** It strikes a balance between robust security measures and user-friendliness, ensuring that security does not come at the expense of usability.

Disadvantages of Security by Design
1. **Increased Complexity:** Incorporating security measures may add complexity to the system's design, potentially making it more challenging to implement and manage.

2. **Potential Over-Engineering:** Overemphasis on security can lead to over-engineering, potentially hindering performance, and efficiency.

3. **Time and Resource Constraints:** Implementing Security by Design requires dedicated time and expertise, which may not always be readily available, especially in fast-paced development environments.

4. **Evolving Threat Landscape:** Security measures need to be continuously updated and adapted to stay effective against emerging threats, requiring ongoing vigilance and resources.

5. **Potential Usability Challenges:** Overly strict security measures can inconvenience users, potentially leading to resistance or workarounds that may compromise security.

1.4 The Human Element in Cybersecurity

In the intricate dance of cybersecurity, the human factor emerges as a linchpin in the efficacy of defences. While technology provides the robust infrastructure, it is the people behind the screens who wield the power to bolster or inadvertently undermine the security of an organisation.

First Line of Defence

In the digital realm, employees stand as the first line of defence against potential cyber threats. Their actions, from crafting resilient passwords to promptly identifying and reporting suspicious activities, fortify the walls of an organisation's cyber fortress. Conversely, uninformed, or negligent behaviour can introduce chinks in this armour, leaving sensitive data and systems vulnerable to exploitation.

A Potential Vulnerability

Yet, in this paradoxical dynamic, humans also stand as a potential vulnerability. The art of deception, known as social engineering, preys on human psychology, manipulating trust and exploiting human tendencies. In an era of increasing sophistication, cybercriminals craft convincing narratives, coaxing individuals into unwittingly divulging sensitive information or executing malicious actions.

Mitigating Human-Related Risks

The art of cybersecurity transcends codes and algorithms. It extends into the realm of human behaviour, education, and awareness. To fortify this vital aspect, organisations must cultivate a culture of security consciousness.

Comprehensive Training and Awareness Programs

Empowering employees with the knowledge and skills to recognize and respond to potential threats is paramount. Regular, comprehensive training programs equip individuals with the tools to identify phishing attempts, secure their passwords, and navigate the digital landscape securely. These initiatives serve as a bulwark against the ever-evolving tactics of cyber adversaries.

Cultivating a Culture of Security Consciousness

Beyond training, instilling a culture of security consciousness is imperative. This encompasses fostering an environment where cybersecurity is not viewed as a hindrance but as a collective responsibility. Encouraging open communication channels for reporting potential threats and providing recognition for vigilant behaviour contributes to a resilient security posture.

Conclusion

In the symphony of cybersecurity, the human element harmonises with technology to create a robust defence against digital threats. Acknowledging the pivotal role of individuals, and investing in their education and awareness, fortifies an organisation's security posture. Through this synergy, organisations can navigate the digital frontier with confidence and resilience.

1.5 The Cybersecurity Landscape Today: Navigating Complexity and Innovation

In the dynamic theatre of cybersecurity, the current landscape unfurls before us as a tapestry woven with threads of innovation and challenge. The adversaries that prowl this digital domain are more sophisticated and resourceful than ever before, weaving intricate webs of threats that span the global network. To comprehend and combat these forces, one must first acquaint themselves with the prevailing trends and phenomena that shape our contemporary cybersecurity landscape.

Advanced Persistent Threats (APTs): A Stealthy Menace

At the forefront of modern cyber threats stand Advanced Persistent Threats, or APTs. These highly orchestrated, covert attacks are characterised by their persistent and stealthy nature. Adversaries, often state-sponsored or organized crime groups, employ advanced techniques to infiltrate and dwell within networks for extended periods. Their aims may range from data theft to espionage, underscoring the need for vigilant and sophisticated defence mechanisms.

Ransomware: The Digital Extortionist

Ransomware, a malevolent breed of malware, has emerged as a prominent threat vector. This insidious software encrypts critical data, holding it hostage until a ransom is paid. The consequences of a successful ransomware attack can be catastrophic, leading to disrupted operations, financial losses, and reputational damage.

Zero-Day Vulnerabilities: The Silent Threats

Zero-day vulnerabilities are akin to hidden traps in the digital landscape. These are software flaws that remain undisclosed to the vendor, providing a window of opportunity for cybercriminals to exploit them before a patch or update is released. Mitigating this threat requires a combination of vigilant monitoring, rapid response, and proactive vulnerability management.

State-Sponsored Cyber Espionage: Geopolitical Intrigue

In the realm of international relations, cyberspace has become a battleground for state-sponsored espionage campaigns. Governments engage in covert digital operations to gather intelligence, disrupt adversaries, or exert influence. The sophistication and scope of these operations underscore the geopolitical implications of cybersecurity.

Internet of Things (IoT): Expanding the Attack Surface

The proliferation of Internet of Things devices has expanded the attack surface, introducing new vectors for potential compromise. From smart thermostats to industrial control systems, these interconnected devices offer both convenience and complexity, necessitating robust security measures to safeguard against potential vulnerabilities.

AI and ML: The Double-Edged Sword

Artificial Intelligence (AI) and Machine Learning (ML) have emerged as game-changing technologies in cybersecurity. They reinforce threat detection, automating responses and augmenting human capabilities. However, they also present new challenges, as cybercriminals seek to exploit and deceive AI-powered systems.

Understanding this multifaceted cybersecurity landscape is paramount for developing effective defence strategies. It requires a synthesis of vigilance, adaptability, and technological innovation. As we traverse this digital frontier, armed with knowledge and strategic acumen, we fortify our organisations against the evolving threats that shape our interconnected world.

Chapter 2: Navigating Cybersecurity Frameworks

Learning Outcomes
- **2.1 – Understand Cyber Threat Intelligence**
    - Identify key concepts of cyber threat intelligence.
    - Explain the following terms in relation to cybersecurity:
        - threats • exploits • vulnerabilities • risk.
    - Describe the threat intelligence lifecycle.
    - Describe how to find out about emerging attack techniques and how to recognise them.
    - Consider what could be included in Open-Source Intelligence (OSINT) data sets.
    - Explain why it is important to only use reliable and valid sources of Open-Source Intelligence information.
    - Explain the importance of using reliable sources of information in relation to cybersecurity threats.
    - Consider the current threat status and make possible recommendations based upon cyber threat intelligence (CTI) information.
    - Analyse relevant cyber threat intelligence information requirements for an organisation
- **2.2 - Understand threat models.**
    - Describe a range of threat models.
    - Explain the steps within a threat model.
    - Evaluate a threat model.
- **2.3 - Understand malicious software.**
    - Identify types of malicious software.
    - Describe the effects of different types of malicious software on an infected system.
    - Describe the motives for using specific malicious software attacks.
    - Identify how specific malicious software attacks are made more effective due to human factors.
- **2.4 - Know about Social Engineering**
    - Explain the term 'social engineering'.
    - Give examples of how Open-Source Intelligence can be used for social engineering.
    - Describe ways a social engineering attack could take place.

2. Introduction

In this comprehensive chapter, readers are immersed in the intricate landscape of cyber threats and the corresponding defence mechanisms crucial for safeguarding organisational assets. The journey begins with an exploration of threat modelling, providing a structured approach to identifying vulnerabilities and critical assets. The step-by-step process encompasses scope definition, data collection, threat identification, risk assessment, mitigation strategies, monitoring, response planning, and continuous review.

Moving forward, the chapter delves into the evaluation of threat models within the realm of threat intelligence. Readers gain insights into factors such as data accuracy, coverage, timeliness, actionability, and collaboration, ensuring the effectiveness and reliability of threat models.

The narrative seamlessly transitions to understanding malicious software, where various categories, including viruses, worms, Trojans, ransomware, and spyware, are dissected. Techniques and tactics employed by malicious software are explored, shedding light on the diverse impacts on compromised systems and emphasizing the significance of detection and mitigation.

A highlight of the chapter is a series of case studies, featuring a notorious malware attack—CovidLock. This real-world example dissects the attack's methods, impacts, and lessons learned, providing valuable insights into defending against similar threats. Additionally, the discussion delves into how human factors contribute to the effectiveness of malicious software attacks, emphasizing the role of social engineering.

The chapter then takes a deep dive into social engineering, unravelling the psychology behind the manipulation of human behaviour for nefarious purposes. From principles of persuasion to manipulation techniques and influence strategies, readers gain a profound understanding of the tactics employed by social engineers. Practical advice and best practices are provided to defend against social engineering attacks, emphasizing the importance of awareness, education, and technical safeguards.

Concluding the chapter is a detailed exploration of common social engineering techniques, including phishing, pretexting, tailgating, and baiting. Mitigation strategies are outlined, emphasizing the need for a security-conscious culture, robust authentication, and regular security assessments.

Chapter 2 serves as a comprehensive guide, equipping readers with the knowledge and tools necessary to navigate and defend against the dynamic and evolving landscape of cyber threats.

2.1 Understand Cyber Threat Intelligence

Cyber Threat Intelligence (CTI) forms the bedrock of a robust cybersecurity strategy. It encompasses the gathering of data and insights about potential cyber threats, the actors behind them, their motives, techniques, and targets. This intelligence gathering and analysis serve as a crucial proactive measure in safeguarding digital assets.

The process involves the collection, analysis, and interpretation of data, unravelling the tactics, techniques, and procedures (TTPs) employed by threat actors in the digital realm. By distilling this information, organisations gain essential context and actionable intelligence, which in turn empowers them to make informed decisions, bolster their security measures, and proactively mitigate potential risks.

Scenario

Consider a recent house break-in and theft in your community. The police visited the scene and are trying to build information (intelligence) on this new threat; you have been summoned by police to work with them to support their actions and report gathering.

In groups of 3:
1. Identify possible ideas to help understand the threat.
2. Explain each idea identified.

2.1.1 Key Aspects of Cyber Threat Intelligence (CTI)

This section delves into the fundamental concepts of Cyber Threat Intelligence (CTI). It explores the nature of threat intelligence, its purpose, and the various elements that constitute an effective CTI program. By grasping these key concepts, readers will gain a solid foundation in understanding and utilising threat intelligence to strengthen their cybersecurity defences.

Data Collection

CTI hinges on the meticulous collection of data from diverse sources. These include open-source intelligence (OSINT), closed forums, malware analysis, security incident reports, and collaborative efforts with trusted partners and industry-sharing communities. The gathered data encompasses indicators of compromise (IOCs) such as IP addresses, domains, hashes, and patterns associated with malicious activities.

This comprehensive approach to data collection ensures a wide net is cast, allowing for a nuanced understanding of emerging threats.

Analysis and Contextualisation

The collected data undergoes rigorous analysis and contextualisation. This process seeks to unearth patterns, discern trends, and identify potential correlations. By connecting disparate data points, threat actors, their methodologies, infrastructure, and intentions begin to crystallise.

This phase is akin to fitting together pieces of a puzzle, revealing the bigger picture of cyber threats.

Threat Actor Profiling

CTI involves constructing profiles of threat actors and delving into their motivations. These actors can range from cybercriminal organisations to nation-state entities, hacktivists, or even internal threats. The profiling process includes understanding their capabilities, preferred techniques, historical attacks, and choice of targets.

Understanding the motivations and methods of threat actors is akin to knowing your adversaries on the digital battlefield.

Incident Response and Mitigation

CTI provides a real-time or near-real-time stream of information about emerging threats and ongoing attacks. This empowers organisations to take proactive measures in detecting, containing, and responding to security incidents effectively.

Having this intelligence at hand is akin to seeing the storm brewing before it hits, allowing for timely action.

Strategic Planning

CTI serves as the foundation for informed strategic planning. By identifying emerging threats and industry-specific risks, organisations can chart long-term security strategies. This includes resource allocation and prioritisation of security initiatives, all guided by intelligence-driven insights.

Strategic planning informed by CTI is akin to setting the course of a ship with a clear map of potential dangers.

Collaboration and Sharing

Encouraging collaboration and information sharing among organisations, security researchers, and government agencies is a vital aspect of CTI. This collective defence approach enhances situational awareness and strengthens the cybersecurity community's ability to combat threats.

In a digital ecosystem, shared intelligence is akin to building a network of watchtowers, collectively guarding against potential threats.

2.1.2 Describe the Threat Intelligence Lifecycle

Threat Intelligence Lifecycle

The threat intelligence lifecycle serves as a structured framework for the collection, analysis, and application of cyber threat intelligence. It outlines the stages involved in transforming raw data into actionable insights that inform proactive cybersecurity measures. The threat intelligence lifecycle outlines the stages involved in the *collection*, *analysis*, and *utilisation* of cyber threat intelligence.

1. Planning and Direction

This inaugural phase entails setting clear objectives, defining priorities, and establishing the framework for the threat intelligence program. It involves scoping intelligence requirements, determining sources for monitoring, and establishing measurable goals for program effectiveness.

This phase is akin to charting the course for an intelligence-gathering expedition, defining what needs to be known and why.

2. Data Collection

Relevant data is collected from a wide array of sources, encompassing internal logs, external feeds, open-source intelligence, and collaborative partnerships. This phase may employ automated tools, manual research, or specialised threat intelligence platforms. The data collected includes indicators of compromise (IOCs), security events, threat reports, and other pertinent information.

This phase is akin to gathering pieces of evidence, each contributing to a clearer understanding of potential threats.

3. Processing and Analysis

Collected data is subjected to rigorous processing and analysis to distil meaningful insights and identify potential threats. This involves categorising and correlating data, conducting pattern analysis, and applying contextual information. Techniques such as data mining, machine learning, and human analysis are leveraged to identify trends, patterns, and potential indicators of threats.

In this phase, raw data is refined into valuable intelligence, akin to extracting precious metals from ore.

4. Intelligence Production

The analysed data is transformed into actionable intelligence. This involves creating reports, alerts, and indicators tailored to specific audiences, such as incident response teams, executives, or security analysts. The produced intelligence must be concise, accurate, and directly relevant.

This phase is akin to crafting a clear, detailed map for navigators, ensuring they have the information they need.

5. Dissemination and Sharing

The intelligence is shared with relevant stakeholders, both within the organisation and with trusted external partners or communities. This sharing of intelligence enhances situational awareness, improves incident response capabilities, and fosters collaboration within the cybersecurity community.

Sharing intelligence is akin to distributing a weather report, ensuring everyone is prepared for potential storms.

6. Consumption and Integration

The intelligence is consumed by various teams within the organisation, including incident response, threat hunting, vulnerability management, and security operations. It is integrated into existing security systems, processes, and decision-making frameworks to enhance detection, prevention, and response capabilities.

This phase ensures that intelligence is effectively used to bolster the organisation's security posture, akin to fortifying a castle's defences.

7. Feedback and Evaluation

Establishing feedback loops is essential for gathering insights on the effectiveness and relevance of the threat intelligence. This involves evaluating the impact of the intelligence on security operations, incident response, and overall risk management. The feedback received is used to refine and improve the threat intelligence program.

Feedback and evaluation are akin to reviewing the successes and challenges of a military campaign, learning, and adapting for the future.

8. Continuous Improvement

The threat intelligence lifecycle is an iterative process. Lessons learned and insights gained from previous phases are used to continuously refine and improve the program's effectiveness. This includes updating intelligence requirements, refining collection techniques, and enhancing analysis and dissemination processes.

This phase ensures that the organisation is ever ready and adaptive in the face of evolving threats, akin to an army honing its skills for future battles.

This comprehensive understanding of the Threat Intelligence Lifecycle equips organisations with a structured approach to gathering, analysing, and applying intelligence. By adhering to this lifecycle, organisations can effectively fortify their defences and proactively respond to potential cyber threats.

2.1.3 Unearthing Emerging Attack Techniques

To stay ahead of cyber threats, one must be adept at identifying and understanding emerging attack techniques. This section equips readers with the knowledge and tools necessary to recognise and mitigate evolving threats. Through practical examples and case studies, readers will develop the skills needed to anticipate and respond to the latest attack vectors.

Tutorial Activity

Imagine you work for a cybersecurity company and your manager has asked you to describe how to find out about emerging attack techniques and to state how to recognise them – *what would you say?*

Emerging Attack Techniques

To stay ahead of emerging attack techniques and effectively recognise them, cybersecurity professionals and organisations can employ a range of proactive strategies. Key approaches include:

1. **Stay Updated with Threat Intelligence**

    - Subscribing to threat intelligence feeds, security blogs, and industry publications can provide valuable insights into emerging attack techniques.

    - These sources often share information about the latest vulnerabilities, attack vectors, and tactics used by threat actors.

2. **Monitor Security Research and Reports**

    - Regularly reviewing security research papers, reports, and studies conducted by reputable organisations, security vendors, and research groups is crucial.

    - These publications often highlight emerging threats, attack trends, and new techniques being utilised in the wild.

3. **Participate in Security Communities**

    - Engaging in online security communities, forums, and mailing lists where security professionals share information and discuss emerging threats is highly beneficial.

    - Active participation allows for knowledge exchange, sharing of experiences, and learning from the experiences of others.

4. **Follow Security Conferences and Events**

    - Attending cybersecurity conferences, seminars, and webinars is essential, as experts often present their findings on the latest attack techniques.

    - These events provide opportunities to network, learn from experts, and gain insights into emerging threats.

5. **Engage in Threat Hunting**

    - Adopt proactive threat hunting practices within your organisation. Actively search for signs of compromise, anomalous behaviour, or indicators of emerging attack techniques within your network and systems.

    - This can involve leveraging security tools, conducting log analysis, and using behavioural analytics to identify potential threats.

6. **Analyse Incident Reports and Case Studies**

    - Study incident reports, post-mortem analyses, and case studies of security breaches.

    - These resources often provide detailed information about the attack techniques, tools, and methods employed by threat actors.

    - By analysing past incidents, patterns and trends can be identified to help recognise emerging attack techniques.

7. **Maintain Strong Relationships with the Security Community**

    - Foster relationships with trusted peers, security vendors, researchers, and industry experts. Engaging in information-sharing initiatives, collaborative research projects, or participating in vulnerability disclosure programs can provide early access to information about emerging threats.

8. **Continuous Learning and Skill Development**

    - Invest in ongoing education and training for cybersecurity professionals within your organisation. Encourage them to stay updated with the latest attack techniques, security trends, and defensive strategies through certifications, workshops, and relevant courses.

By combining these strategies, cybersecurity professionals can proactively seek out and recognise emerging attack techniques, ensuring their organisations remain vigilant and well-prepared in the face of evolving threats.

2.1.4 Open-Source Intelligence (OSINT) Data Sets

What could be included in the Open-Source Intelligence (OSINT) data sets?

Open-Source Intelligence (OSINT) refers to information collected from publicly available sources. The data sets used in OSINT can encompass a wide array of information, each providing a unique window into various aspects of individuals, organisations, events, and trends, such as:

1. **Social Media**
    - OSINT data sets often include information gathered from social media platforms. This can range from individual posts and comments to entire profiles and public conversations. Such data can offer profound insights into the behaviours, affiliations, and sentiments of users, as well as trends and emerging discussions.

2. Websites and Blogs

- Information collected from publicly accessible websites, blogs, forums, and online publications constitutes a vital part of OSINT data sets. This category encompasses articles, reports, whitepapers, and any publicly available content that can offer valuable information. It provides a wealth of knowledge on diverse subjects.

3. Public Records

- OSINT data sets may incorporate data from official public records. These include information from government databases, court records, property records, business registrations, and other legally accessible sources. Such records can furnish details about individuals, organisations, and their activities, helping to establish a comprehensive profile.

4. News Sources

- News articles, press releases, and media coverage serve as invaluable sources of information for OSINT. Regularly monitoring news sources is essential for understanding current events, incidents, and trends that may have relevance to a particular investigation or intelligence-gathering endeavour.

5. Academic Research

- Academic publications, research papers, and dissertations contribute significantly to OSINT data sets. These sources often provide in-depth analysis, insights, and findings that are publicly available. They can be particularly useful for comprehending complex subjects and emerging technologies.

6. Government Reports and Publications

- Information published by government agencies holds immense value in OSINT. This category includes reports, policies, regulations, and statistics, which can illuminate various subjects, including national security, crime, economics, public health, and more. These documents often contain authoritative information.

7. Publicly Available Data Sets

- Various organisations and institutions make certain datasets publicly available. These can encompass a wide range of information, such as demographic data, weather data, economic data, transportation data, and more. Analysing these datasets can yield valuable insights into specific aspects of interest, aiding in decision-making and trend analysis.

By leveraging these diverse sources of information, OSINT practitioners can compile comprehensive data sets that provide critical intelligence for a wide range of applications, from cybersecurity to investigative journalism and beyond. The combination of these sources enriches the depth and breadth of insights that OSINT can offer.

2.1.5 The Imperative of Reliable OSINT Sources

Using reliable and valid sources of Open-Source Intelligence (OSINT) information is paramount for maintaining the accuracy and credibility of intelligence analysis.

In the ever-evolving landscape of cybersecurity, the reliability of Open-Source Intelligence (OSINT) sources stands as a cornerstone in the pursuit of accurate and trustworthy intelligence. This section delves into the critical importance of drawing information from valid and reputable sources when engaging in OSINT activities. Here, readers will gain a comprehensive understanding of why discerning reliable information is paramount for sound decision-making and threat assessment.

Why it is important to only use reliable and valid sources of Open-Source Intelligence information?

Why Reliability Matters

Below are several key reasons highlighting the critical importance of this practice:

1. Accuracy and Reliability
- Relying on sources with established credibility ensures that the information gathered is accurate and trustworthy. Valid sources have robust verification processes and adhere to ethical standards, significantly reducing the risk of encountering misinformation, false data, or biased content that could otherwise compromise the integrity of the intelligence analysis.

2. Quality of Analysis
- The quality of intelligence analysis is heavily contingent upon the quality of the source material. Utilising valid sources with accurate and reliable information bolsters the integrity and effectiveness of the analysis. This, in turn, leads to more informed decision-making, as the conclusions drawn are based on a solid foundation of verifiable data.

3. Reputation and Trust
- Employing reliable sources serves to uphold the reputation and trustworthiness of both the intelligence analysts and the organisations they represent. Citing and referencing valid sources not only substantiates the findings but also strengthens the credibility of the intelligence products. This, in turn, fosters trust with stakeholders, as they have confidence in the rigor of the analysis.

4. Legal and Ethical Considerations
- Utilising reliable sources ensures compliance with legal and ethical frameworks governing information gathering and dissemination. It minimises the risk of using unauthorised or illegally obtained information, safeguarding both the integrity of the intelligence analysis and the rights of individuals or organisations involved. Adhering to ethical standards also promotes transparency and accountability in the intelligence process.

5. Risk Mitigation
- Valid sources play a pivotal role in mitigating the risk of relying on false or misleading information. Engaging with reputable sources reduces the potential for critical errors, misinterpretation of data, or drawing incorrect conclusions. Properly vetting sources is an essential safeguard against formulating flawed strategies or taking misguided actions based on flawed intelligence.

6. Reputation Damage Control
- If inaccurate or unreliable information is used in intelligence analysis and subsequently disseminated, it can have severe repercussions for the reputation of the intelligence analysts and the organisation at large. This can impact not only credibility but also partnerships, customer relationships, and the overall trust in the intelligence process. Using valid sources is a critical step in ensuring that the intelligence produced is of the highest quality and reliability.

2.1.6 Practical Guidelines and Best Practices

To discern reliable information from potentially misleading or false data, practitioners should employ a set of practical guidelines and best practices. By adhering to these guidelines, practitioners can navigate the OSINT landscape with confidence, honing their ability to distinguish between trustworthy information and potentially misleading data. This, in turn, empowers them to provide reliable and accurate intelligence outputs that contribute to informed decision-making and strategic planning in the realm of cybersecurity.

These guidelines and best practices include:
1. **Source Verification**: Cross-verify information from multiple trusted and reputable sources to corroborate its accuracy and authenticity.

2. **Check for Attribution**: Ensure that the source provides clear attribution and references for the information provided.

3. **Evaluate Source Expertise**: Assess the expertise and credibility of the source based on its track record, reputation, and domain of expertise.

4. **Consider Peer Review and Citations**: Prioritize information from sources that have undergone peer review or have been cited by reputable experts or organisations.

5. **Stay Informed of Source Updates**: Keep abreast of updates and revisions made by reliable sources to their published information.

2.1.7 The Anchoring Role of Reliable Sources

Reliable sources form the bedrock of effective intelligence analysis, particularly in the realm of cybersecurity threat assessments. This section underscores the criticality of leveraging trustworthy information to produce accurate and dependable intelligence outputs. By doing so, readers will be empowered to contribute to informed decision-making and strategic planning in the face of evolving cyber threats.

Introduction

Using reliable sources of information is paramount in understanding and addressing cybersecurity threats. In the dynamic landscape of cyber threats, accurate and current information is indispensable for making informed decisions, implementing effective security measures, and mitigating potential risks.

Below are some crucial reasons why placing trust in reliable sources is paramount in the realm of cybersecurity threats:

1. Accuracy of Information
- Reliable sources furnish accurate and verified information about cybersecurity threats. This information is derived from rigorous research, data analysis, and expert insights, ensuring its trustworthiness and credibility. This accuracy is fundamental for comprehending the nature, tactics, and potential impact of various threats.

2. Timeliness
- Cyber threats can emerge and evolve swiftly, necessitating timely information to stay ahead of potential risks. Reliable sources often provide real-time updates on emerging threats, vulnerabilities, and attacks. This empowers organisations and individuals to promptly respond and adapt their security strategies to counteract new or evolving threats.

3. Depth of Analysis
- Reliable sources frequently offer in-depth analysis of cybersecurity threats, providing a deeper understanding of the motives, techniques, and potential consequences of various attacks. This analysis aids organisations and individuals in gaining insights into the underlying patterns and trends of cyber threats, enabling them to develop proactive measures and preventive strategies.

4. Trustworthiness
- Trustworthy sources have a track record of accuracy and reliability, establishing trust among users. Relying on such sources helps prevent the dissemination of misinformation or unverified claims, which could lead to confusion, panic, or inappropriate countermeasures. Trustworthy sources often have established expertise and a consistent history of providing accurate and reliable information over time.

5. Comprehensive Coverage
- Reliable sources encompass a broad spectrum of cybersecurity threats, including different attack vectors, vulnerabilities, malware, hacking techniques, and emerging trends. Consulting such sources enables individuals and organisations to gain comprehensive knowledge about the ever-evolving threat landscape and ensure their security measures address the full spectrum of potential risks.

6. Industry Standards and Best Practices
- Reliable sources often furnish information on industry standards, frameworks, and best practices for cybersecurity. These sources serve as guides for organisations in implementing effective security measures, establishing robust policies, and adopting proactive strategies to protect their systems, networks, and data.

7. Regulatory Compliance
- Regulatory bodies and government agencies frequently publish reliable information and guidelines related to cybersecurity threats. Complying with these regulations is crucial for organisations to ensure the security and privacy of their digital assets. Relying on trusted sources helps organisations stay informed about the latest regulatory requirements and maintain compliance.

By prioritising the use of reliable sources, intelligence analysts can fortify their analyses, providing stakeholders with actionable and well-founded insights to navigate the complex landscape of cybersecurity threats. This, in turn, contributes to a more resilient and secure digital environment.

2.1.8 Current Threat Status and Recommendations

Staying well-informed about the dynamic threat landscape is paramount for maintaining effective cybersecurity. This section imparts valuable guidance on assessing the present threat status and formulating tailored recommendations based on up-to-date cyber threat intelligence. Readers will acquire the skills needed to adapt their security measures to address the most pertinent and timely threats.

Introduction: Cybersecurity stands as an ever-evolving challenge in today's interconnected digital landscape. With cloud computing, networks, data, and infrastructure constantly at risk, real-time access to current cyber threat intelligence is imperative. This can be likened to how we track the threat status of phenomena like the COVID-19 pandemic or sexually transmitted diseases. What is the current threat status? What are the recommended strategies based on available threat intelligence?

However, it's important to acknowledge that the most recent threat status or specific recommendations based on the very latest cyber threat intelligence may not always be immediately accessible. Nevertheless, based on studies and information available as of September 2021, some general recommendations can be provided to reinforce cybersecurity posture.

2.1.9 General Recommendations to Enhance Cybersecurity Posture

1. **Keep Software Up to Date**
    - Regularly update your operating system, antivirus software, web browsers, and other applications. This ensures you have the latest security patches and defences against known vulnerabilities.

2. **Use Strong, Unique Passwords**
    - Create robust passwords for all online accounts. Consider using a password manager to securely store them. Avoid reusing passwords across multiple accounts.

3. **Enable Multi-Factor Authentication (MFA)**
    - MFA provides an extra layer of security by requiring an additional verification step, such as a fingerprint scan or a one-time code sent to your mobile device, in addition to a password.

4. **Be Cautious of Phishing Attempts**
    - Exercise caution when dealing with emails, messages, or websites that request personal information or contain suspicious links. Verify the legitimacy of the source before clicking on any links or providing sensitive information.

5. **Regularly Back Up Your Data**
    - Create regular backups of your important files and verify that the backups are successful. This can help you recover your data in case of a ransomware attack or other data loss incidents.

6. **Educate Yourself and Your Team**
    - Stay well-informed about the latest cybersecurity threats and best practices. Provide cybersecurity training to employees and foster a culture of security awareness within your organisation.

7. **Implement Network Security Measures**
    - Employ firewalls, intrusion detection and prevention systems, and secure network configurations to shield your network from unauthorised access.

8. **Conduct Regular Security Assessments**
    - Perform vulnerability scans, penetration tests, and security audits to identify and rectify potential weaknesses in your systems.

9. **Establish an Incident Response Plan**
    - Develop a documented plan outlining the steps to be taken in the event of a cyber incident. This will help minimise the impact and facilitate a coordinated response.

10. **Engage with Cybersecurity Professionals**
    - Consider seeking guidance from cybersecurity experts or hiring a reputable cybersecurity firm to assess your organisation's security posture and provide tailored recommendations.

By following these general recommendations, individuals and organisations can significantly enhance their cybersecurity posture, making them more resilient to the evolving landscape of cyber threats. Remember, while these recommendations offer a solid foundation, it's essential to stay vigilant and adapt to emerging threats as they arise.

2.1.10 Tailoring Intelligence for Your Organisation

Every organisation possesses unique cybersecurity needs. This section serves as a guide for readers to discern and customise cyber threat intelligence information according to their organisation's specific requirements. By comprehending the distinctive characteristics of their environment, readers will be empowered to formulate targeted and effective cybersecurity strategies.

Introduction

To proficiently analyse pertinent cyber threat intelligence information for an organisation, it is imperative to pinpoint the specific requirements and priorities based on the organisation's industry, size, threat landscape, and security objectives. Some key requirements to consider are:

1. Industry-Specific Threats
- Different industries confront distinct cyber threats. Tailoring the intelligence collection and analysis process based on the specific threats targeting the organisation's industry is paramount. For instance, financial institutions may contend with threats like phishing, account takeover, or payment fraud, while healthcare organisations may be targeted by ransomware or data breaches.

2. External Threat Actors
- Identifying the threat actors that pose a significant risk to the organisation is crucial. This may encompass nation-state actors, organised cybercriminal groups, hacktivists, or insider threats. Understanding their tactics, techniques, and motivations aids in prioritising intelligence requirements and implementing appropriate defences.
- *Note: Honeypots are decoy systems or networks designed to lure attackers and gather information about their methods and objectives. They can be a valuable tool in understanding the tactics and techniques of threat actors.*

3. Threat Intelligence Sources
- Determine the sources of threat intelligence most pertinent to the organisation. These may encompass open-source intelligence (OSINT), commercial threat intelligence feeds, sector-specific information sharing communities, government alerts, or information from trusted cybersecurity vendors.

4. Vulnerabilities and Exploits
- Stay abreast of the latest vulnerabilities and exploits relevant to the organisation's infrastructure and software stack. Prioritise intelligence related to vulnerabilities that could be exploited by threat actors and ensure timely patching or mitigation.

5. Emerging Threats and Trends
- Monitor emerging threats, attack techniques, and trends in the cybersecurity landscape. This encompasses keeping track of new malware variants, zero-day exploits, social engineering tactics, or emerging technologies that may introduce new risks.

6. Indicators of Compromise (IOCs)
- Identify the IOCs that are most pertinent to the organisation, such as malicious IP addresses, domain names, URLs, file hashes, or email addresses associated with known threat actors or malware. Regularly update the organisation's security tools and defences with relevant IOCs to detect and respond to potential threats.

7. Internal Telemetry and Logs
- Leverage internal network and system logs to identify unusual or suspicious activities. Monitor network traffic, user behaviour, access logs, and system events to detect signs of compromise or potential insider threats.

8. Legal and Regulatory Requirements
- Consider the organisation's legal and regulatory obligations regarding data protection and privacy. Stay updated on relevant regulations, such as the General Data Protection Regulation (GDPR) or industry-specific compliance frameworks, to ensure cyber threat intelligence efforts align with these requirements.

9. Incident Response and Recovery Capabilities
- Assess the organisation's incident response and recovery capabilities to determine the specific intelligence requirements needed during an incident. Identify the information needed to understand the scope, nature, and impact of an incident, as well as the intelligence necessary to support effective incident response and recovery efforts.

10. Collaborative Information Sharing
- Participate in information sharing initiatives and collaborate with other organisations within the same industry or sector to exchange threat intelligence. Sharing and receiving intelligence from trusted partners can enhance the organisation's ability to detect and respond to threats effectively.

By tailoring intelligence efforts to these specific requirements, organisations can significantly enhance their ability to proactively address cyber threats that are most pertinent to their unique environment. This targeted approach ensures that resources are optimally allocated to defend against the most relevant risks.

Tutorial Activity

Leveraging Reliable Sources in Cybersecurity

In the dynamic realm of cybersecurity, leveraging reliable sources is paramount for understanding and addressing threats effectively. Here's a brief tutorial to reinforce your understanding:

1. **Importance of Accuracy:** Understand why accurate information is crucial for comprehending the nature, tactics, and potential impact of cybersecurity threats.

2. **Timeliness Matters:** Learn why real-time updates are essential for staying ahead of potential risks and adapting security strategies promptly.

3. **Depth of Analysis:** Explore how in-depth analysis aids in understanding motives, techniques, and consequences of cyber-attacks.

4. **Trustworthiness:** Discover the importance of trusting sources with a proven track record to prevent misinformation and confusion.

5. **Comprehensive Coverage:** Recognise the value of sources that cover a broad spectrum of cybersecurity threats and trends.

6. **Industry Standards and Best Practices:** Gain insights into industry standards and best practices for implementing effective security measures.

7. **Regulatory Compliance:** Understand the significance of staying informed about regulatory requirements to ensure security and privacy compliance.

Quiz: Test Your Understanding

1. Why is accuracy of information crucial in cybersecurity threat assessments?
2. How does timely information help organisations stay ahead of potential risks?
3. What benefits does in-depth analysis offer in understanding cyber threats?
4. Why is trustworthiness important when considering cybersecurity information sources?

5. How does comprehensive coverage of cybersecurity threats contribute to better security strategies?

6. What role do industry standards and best practices play in cybersecurity?

7. Why is it essential for organisations to stay informed about regulatory requirements?

2.2 Understand Threat Models
2.2.1 The Essence of Threat Modelling

In this section, readers will delve into the fundamental concept of threat modelling, which serves as a proactive strategy for recognizing and countering potential security risks. The chapter will guide readers in systematically examining systems, applications, and processes, enabling them to foresee and fortify against a spectrum of potential threat scenarios. This proactive approach empowers individuals and organisations to take pre-emptive measures, ultimately strengthening their overall cybersecurity posture.

Introduction - *explanation*

Threat intelligence threat models involve understanding and predicting potential cyber threats and attacks. They help organisations proactively identify and respond to emerging risks.

The following are examples of threat intelligence threat models:

1. **Adversary-centric Models**
    - These models focus on understanding the capabilities, motivations, and tactics of specific threat actors or groups.
    - They analyse their targets, attack patterns, and historical data to anticipate future actions.

2. **Indicator-based Models**
    - Indicator-based threat models rely on specific indicators of compromise (IOCs) or observable patterns to detect threats.
    - These models leverage threat intelligence feeds, such as IP addresses, domain names, malware signatures, or behavioural patterns associated with known threats.

3. Risk-based Models
- Risk-based threat models assess the likelihood and impact of potential threats based on contextual factors, such as the organisation's industry, assets, vulnerabilities, and historical attack data.
- They prioritise threats based on their potential risk to the organisation.

4. Kill Chain Models
- Kill chain models map out the different stages of a cyber-attack, from initial reconnaissance to the final objective.
- By understanding each stage, organisations can identify potential defensive measures and focus on disrupting the attack at critical points.

5. MITRE ATT&CK Framework
- The MITRE ATT&CK (Adversarial Tactics, Techniques, and Common Knowledge) framework provides a comprehensive model of adversary behaviour and techniques.
- It categorises attack techniques and tactics to help organisations understand potential threats and plan their defences accordingly.

6. Zero-Day Exploit Models
- These models focus on identifying and analysing vulnerabilities that are unknown or have not yet been patched by software vendors.
- They involve monitoring and researching emerging threats, exploits, and vulnerabilities to provide early warning and defence strategies.

7. STRIDE
- STRIDE is a threat modelling framework that helps identify and categorise potential threats in a system.
- It stands for *Spoofing, Tampering, Repudiation, Information Disclosure, Denial of Service,* and *Elevation of Privilege.*
    - **Spoofing:** This refers to an attacker impersonating someone or something else, such as faking an identity or IP address.
    - **Tampering:** It involves unauthorised modification or alteration of data or systems, including changing settings or injecting malicious code.
    - **Repudiation:** This threat involves an attacker denying their actions or transactions, making it difficult to hold them accountable.

- **Information Disclosure:** It pertains to the unauthorised exposure or leakage of sensitive information.
- **Denial of Service (DoS):** It involves disrupting or disabling legitimate access to services, systems, or networks.
- **Elevation of Privilege:** This threat involves an attacker gaining higher privileges or unauthorised access to sensitive resources.

8. PASTA (Process for Attack Simulation and Threat Analysis)

- PASTA is an acronym for *Process* for *Attack Simulation* and *Threat Analysis*.
- It is a risk-centric threat modelling methodology that helps identify, analyse, and prioritise potential threats.
- PASTA consists of several steps, including:
    - Planning and scoping the analysis.
    - Assessing the business impact and security objectives.
    - Identifying threats through brainstorming and analysing attack paths.
    - Creating attack simulations and defining attack patterns.
    - Estimating the likelihood and impact of each attack.
    - Prioritising threats based on risk factors.
    - Developing mitigation strategies and countermeasures.

9. LINDDUN (Linkability, Identifiability, Non-repudiation, Detectability, Disclosure of information, Unawareness, Non-compliance)

- LINDDUN is a threat modelling framework developed by Microsoft.
- It stands for *Linkability, Identifiability, Non-repudiation, Detectability, Disclosure of information, Unawareness,* and *Non-compliance*.
    - **Linkability:** It involves an attacker connecting seemingly unrelated information to identify patterns or relationships.
    - **Identifiability:** This threat refers to an attacker being able to uniquely identify individuals or systems.
    - **Non-repudiation:** It ensures that actions or transactions cannot be denied by the involved parties.

- **Detectability:** It pertains to an attacker's ability to perform malicious activities without being detected.
- **Disclosure of information:** This threat involves unauthorised exposure or leakage of sensitive information.
- **Unawareness:** It refers to a lack of awareness or understanding of security threats and risks.
- **Non-compliance:** This threat relates to violations of regulations, standards, or policies.

10. CVSS (Common Vulnerability Scoring System)

- CVSS, which stands for *Common Vulnerability Scoring System*, is a framework used to assess and rate the severity of vulnerabilities in software or systems.
- It provides a standard methodology for assigning numerical scores to vulnerabilities based on various factors, including their impact and exploitability.
- CVSS scores range from 0 to 10, with a higher score indicating a more severe vulnerability.
- The scores are categorised into three levels: low (0.0-3.9), medium (4.0-6.9), and high (7.0-10.0).
- The system considers factors such as attack vector, attack complexity, privilege requirements, and impact on confidentiality, integrity, and availability.

11. Attack Trees

- An attack tree is a graphical representation of a systematic and hierarchical decomposition of possible attacks against a target system.
- It helps in understanding the various steps and paths an attacker might take to exploit vulnerabilities or achieve specific objectives.
- An attack tree consists of nodes and branches that represent different attack steps and the relationships between them.
- The root node represents the primary objective of the attack, while the leaf nodes represent the individual actions or conditions necessary to achieve the objective.

By analysing an attack tree, security professionals can identify potential vulnerabilities, evaluate the likelihood of specific attacks, and develop appropriate mitigation strategies.

These threat modelling frameworks and methodologies provide valuable tools for assessing and addressing potential cyber threats and vulnerabilities in systems or software applications.

2.2.2 Identifying Vulnerabilities and Assets

Understanding an organisation's vulnerabilities and assets is foundational to effective threat modelling. This section guides readers through the process of cataloguing and assessing vulnerabilities, as well as identifying critical assets that require special protection.

Steps within a Threat Model

The steps involved in developing a threat model within the realm of threat intelligence can be summarised as follows:

1. **Scope Definition**
   - Clearly define the scope of the threat model, including the target assets, systems, networks, or applications.
   - Determine the specific objectives of the threat model and the level of intensity required.

2. **Data Collection**
   - Gather relevant data from internal and external sources to inform the threat model.
   - This can include threat intelligence feeds, security incident reports, vulnerability databases, threat actor profiles, and industry-specific information.

3. **Threat Identification**
   - Analyse the collected data to identify potential threats and attack vectors relevant to the scope.
   - This involves understanding the tactics, techniques, and tools employed by threat actors, as well as their motives and targets.

4. **Risk Assessment**
    - Assess the potential impact and likelihood of each identified threat based on the organisation's assets, vulnerabilities, and security controls.
    - Quantify the risks associated with each threat, considering factors such as potential financial loss, reputational damage, or operational disruptions.

5. **Mitigation Strategies**
    - Develop strategies and countermeasures to mitigate the identified threats.
    - This involves selecting appropriate security controls, implementing security best practices, and prioritising actions based on risk levels.

6. **Monitoring and Detection**
    - Define and implement mechanisms for continuous monitoring and threat detection.
    - This may involve deploying intrusion detection systems, security information and event management (SIEM) solutions, or threat intelligence platforms to identify and respond to potential threats in real-time.

7. **Response Planning**
    - Develop an incident response plan to guide the organisation's actions in the event of a cyber-attack.
    - This plan should include predefined procedures, communication protocols, and escalation paths to minimise the impact of an incident.

8. **Review and Update**
    - Regularly review and update the threat model to incorporate new threats, vulnerabilities, or changes in the organisation's environment.
    - Maintain an iterative approach to ensure the threat model remains relevant and effective.

2.2.3 Evaluating Risk and Prioritising Defences

Once vulnerabilities and assets are identified, risk evaluation and prioritisation become crucial. This section explains methodologies for assessing and quantifying risk, enabling organisations to allocate resources strategically to address the most critical threats.

Evaluating a Threat Model

Evaluating a threat model within the realm of threat intelligence is crucial to ensure its effectiveness and reliability.

Some factors to consider when evaluating a threat model includes:
- Data Accuracy and Validity
    - Assess the quality and reliability of the data used to develop the threat model.
    - Evaluate the sources of information, the credibility of the threat intelligence feeds, and the methodologies employed to collect and analyse data.
- Coverage and Context
    - Evaluate the extent to which the threat model covers relevant threats, attack techniques, and threat actors.
    - Consider the comprehensiveness and specificity of the model in addressing the organisation's specific context, industry, and assets.
- Timeliness
    - Determine how up-to-date the threat model is in terms of reflecting current and emerging threats.
    - Evaluate the model's ability to adapt to evolving tactics, techniques, and procedures employed by threat actors.
- Actionability
    - Assess the practicality and feasibility of the recommended mitigation strategies and response plans derived from the threat model.
    - Consider if the model provides actionable insights and guidance that can be effectively implemented to enhance security.
- Feedback and Validation
    - Gather feedback from stakeholders, such as security analysts, incident responders, or threat intelligence analysts, to validate the threat model's accuracy and effectiveness.
    - Compare the model's predictions with actual incidents or emerging threats to evaluate its predictive capabilities.

- Continuous Improvement
    - Evaluate the threat model's ability to adapt and improve over time.
    - Assess if there are mechanisms in place to gather feedback, incorporate lessons learned, and update the model based on new intelligence and emerging threats.
- Collaboration
    - Consider the level of collaboration and involvement of relevant stakeholders, both within the organisation and external parties such as trusted threat intelligence providers.
    - Evaluate if the model incorporates diverse perspectives and expertise to enhance its overall quality and effectiveness.

Tutorial Activity

Exploring Threat Modelling Frameworks

Threat modelling is a proactive strategy for recognising and countering potential security risks. Here, we explore the essence of threat modelling and various frameworks:

1. Adversary-centric Models: Understand specific threat actors' capabilities, motivations, and tactics to anticipate future actions.
2. Indicator-based Models: Rely on specific indicators of compromise (IOCs) or observable patterns to detect threats.
3. Risk-based Models: Assess the likelihood and impact of potential threats based on contextual factors.
4. Kill Chain Models: Map out the different stages of a cyber-attack to identify potential defensive measures.
5. MITRE ATT&CK Framework: Categorise attack techniques and tactics to understand potential threats.
6. Zero-Day Exploit Models: Focus on identifying and analysing vulnerabilities that are unknown or have not yet been patched.
7. STRIDE Framework: Identify and categorize potential threats in a system based on Spoofing, Tampering, Repudiation, etc.

8. PASTA Methodology: Help identify, analyse, and prioritise potential threats through various steps.
9. LINDDUN Framework: Assess threats based on Linkability, Identifiability, Non-repudiation, etc.
10. CVSS: Assess and rate the severity of vulnerabilities in software or systems.
11. Attack Trees: Graphical representation of possible attacks against a target system.

Quiz: Test Your Knowledge on Threat Modelling
1. What does the MITRE ATT&CK framework help organisations understand?
2. How do risk-based threat models assess potential threats?
3. What does the STRIDE framework stand for?
4. Describe the purpose of the PASTA methodology.
5. What does the CVSS framework assess?
6. How do indicator-based threat models detect threats?
7. What is the main purpose of attack trees?

Conclusion

Understanding threat modelling frameworks is essential for organisations to proactively identify and respond to emerging risks effectively. By leveraging these frameworks, organisations can fortify their cybersecurity posture and mitigate potential threats more efficiently.

Use this knowledge to strengthen your organisation's security strategies and adapt to the evolving threat landscape.

2.3 Understand Malicious Software
2.3.1 Categories of Malicious Software

This section provides a comprehensive overview of the different types of malicious software, including viruses, worms, Trojans, ransomware, and spyware. Readers will gain insights into the unique characteristics and behaviours of each category.

Malicious software typically includes:

- **Viruses:** A virus is a program that can replicate itself and spread to other files or systems. It can damage or corrupt files, slow down system performance, and spread to other computers through infected files or networks.

- **Worms:** Worms are like viruses but can spread without any user action. They exploit vulnerabilities in network protocols or operating systems to replicate themselves and spread to other computers. They can consume network bandwidth and cause system instability.

- **Trojans:** Trojans are malicious programs disguised as legitimate software or files. They can create backdoors in a system, allowing remote access to attackers. Trojans often steal sensitive information, such as passwords or credit card details, or provide unauthorised access to the system.

- **Ransomware:** Ransomware encrypts a victim's files or locks them behind a password, making them inaccessible. Attackers demand a ransom in exchange for decrypting or releasing the files. Ransomware can cause significant financial and operational damage to individuals and organisations.

- **Spyware:** Spyware monitors and collects information about a user's activities without their consent. It can track keystrokes, capture screenshots, record browsing habits, and collect personal data. Spyware is often used for targeted advertising, identity theft, or espionage.

- **Adware:** Adware displays unwanted advertisements on a user's computer or mobile device. It can redirect web browsers, slow down system performance, and collect browsing habits to deliver targeted ads. While not inherently malicious, adware can be a nuisance and compromise user privacy.

- **Botnets:** Botnets are networks of infected computers, controlled remotely by an attacker or a command-and-control server. They can be used to launch large-scale attacks, such as Distributed Denial of Service (DDoS) attacks, spread malware, or send spam emails.

2.3.2 Techniques and Tactics of Malicious Software

Understanding the tactics employed by malicious software is key to effective defence. This section delves into the techniques used by malware to infiltrate systems, propagate, and carry out malicious activities, offering readers a deep understanding of their modus operandi.

Impacts of diverse forms of malicious software on a compromised system:

- **Loss or corruption of data:** Many types of malicious software can delete, modify, or encrypt files, resulting in permanent data loss or inaccessibility.

- **System instability:** Malware can consume system resources, slow down performance, or cause frequent crashes and system failures.

- **Unauthorised access and control:** Malicious software like Trojans and botnets can provide attackers with remote access and control over an infected system. Attackers can steal sensitive information, use the system for illegal activities, or launch further attacks.

- **Financial loss:** Ransomware can encrypt files and demand a ransom for their release. Paying the ransom does not guarantee the safe recovery of files, leading to financial losses for individuals and organisations.

- **Privacy breaches:** Spyware and adware can collect personal information without the user's consent. This information can be used for targeted advertising, identity theft, or sold to third parties.

- **Network and internet disruptions:** Worms and botnets can spread across networks, consuming bandwidth, causing network congestion, and disrupting internet connectivity.

2.3.3 Detecting and Mitigating Malware

Detecting and mitigating malware is an ongoing challenge in cybersecurity. This section provides practical strategies and tools for identifying and neutralising malware, including antivirus solutions, intrusion detection systems, and behavioural analysis techniques.

The practical strategies and tools for identifying and neutralising malware encompass a range of approaches. These include the utilisation of robust antivirus solutions, the implementation of effective intrusion detection systems, and the application of behavioural analysis techniques. These tools collectively work towards early detection, swift response, and ultimate removal of malicious software, thereby fortifying the security infrastructure against potential threats.

Reasons behind employing malicious software attacks include:
- **Financial gain:** Many attackers use malware to generate profit. Ransomware, banking Trojans, and credential stealers aim to extract money from individuals or organisations.

- **Espionage and information theft:** Some attackers use malware to gain unauthorised access to sensitive information, such as trade secrets, intellectual property, or classified data.

- **Disruption and sabotage:** Certain malware, like worms or DDoS botnets, can be used to disrupt critical infrastructure, websites, or services, causing inconvenience, financial losses, or reputational damage to the targeted entities.

- **Political or ideological motivations:** Hacktivist groups or state-sponsored actors may deploy malware to advance their political agendas, protest specific actions, or gain leverage in cyber conflicts.

- **Cyber warfare:** Nation-states and military organisations may develop and deploy malware for offensive purposes, such as disrupting enemy networks, conducting surveillance, or sabotaging critical systems.

2.3.4 Case Studies: Notorious Malware Attacks

Real-world case studies offer valuable lessons in cybersecurity. This section examines infamous malware attacks known as CovidLock, dissecting their methods, impacts, and the lessons learned. Readers will gain insights into how organisations can better defend against similar threats.

Case Study Analysis: CovidLock Ransomware Attack

Overview: The CovidLock ransomware attack is a notable example of cybercriminals exploiting fear surrounding the Coronavirus (COVID-19) pandemic. This attack specifically targets Android devices, infecting them through malicious files that falsely promise to provide additional information about the disease.

Attack Details:
1. **Method of Infection**: CovidLock is typically distributed through deceptive files or links that trick users into downloading and installing the malware. These files often masquerade as legitimate sources of COVID-19 information.

2. **Impact on Victims**

    1. *Data Encryption*: Once installed, CovidLock encrypts the data stored on Android devices, making it inaccessible to the victims.

    2. *Ransom Demand*: To regain access to their data, victims are presented with a ransom demand of USD 100 per affected device.

3. **Exploitation of Fear**
   1. *Psychological Manipulation*: Attackers prey on the fear and uncertainty surrounding the pandemic. By promising additional information about COVID-19, they exploit the emotional state of potential victims.

Solutions and Recommendations:
1. **Preventive Measures**
   1. *Education and Awareness*: Educate users about the risks of downloading files or clicking on links from unverified or suspicious sources, especially during times of heightened public concern.
   2. *Install Antivirus Software*: Ensure that devices are equipped with reputable antivirus software capable of detecting and mitigating ransomware threats.

2. **Data Protection**
   1. *Regular Backups*: Encourage users to regularly back up their data to secure and remote locations. This ensures that, in the event of an attack, data can be restored without succumbing to ransom demands.

3. **Incident Response Plan**
   1. *Establish a Response Protocol*: Develop and communicate a clear incident response plan to guide actions in the event of a ransomware attack. This plan should include steps for isolating infected devices, reporting the incident, and seeking professional assistance.

4. **Legal Considerations**
   1. *Report to Authorities*: Encourage victims to report the attack to law enforcement agencies. This can aid in tracking and apprehending cybercriminals.

5. **Security Updates**
   1. *Maintain Device Security*: Ensure that devices receive regular security updates and patches to address known vulnerabilities that could be exploited by ransomware.

Conclusion and Lesson Learned

The CovidLock ransomware attack serves as a stark reminder of the importance of cybersecurity vigilance, especially during times of crisis. By implementing a combination of awareness, preventive measures, and incident response planning, organisations and individuals can significantly reduce the risk posed by such malicious attacks.

How human factors contribute to enhancing the effectiveness of malicious software attacks:

- **Social engineering:** Malware often exploits human vulnerabilities through techniques like phishing emails, fake websites, or enticing downloads. Human factors such as curiosity, trust, or lack of awareness contribute to successful malware infections.

- **Lack of cybersecurity awareness:** Many users have limited knowledge of potential threats and fail to follow secure practices, such as updating software, using strong passwords, or avoiding suspicious websites. This lack of awareness makes them more susceptible to malware attacks.

- **Poor security practices:** Failure to implement proper security measures, such as antivirus software, firewalls, or regular system updates, can make systems more vulnerable to malware infections.

- **Human error:** Mistakes such as clicking on malicious links, opening infected email attachments, or downloading files from untrusted sources can introduce malware to a system.

- **Insider threats:** Malicious software attacks can be facilitated by insiders who have authorised access to systems or networks. These individuals may intentionally introduce malware or compromise security measures for personal gain, revenge, or other motivations.

- Addressing human factors through *education, training*, and *promoting a security-conscious culture* can significantly reduce the effectiveness of malicious software attacks.

2.4 Knowing About Social Engineering
2.4.1 The Psychology of Social Engineering

Understanding the psychological tactics employed by social engineers is essential for effective defence. This section delves into the principles of persuasion, manipulation, and influence that social engineers leverage to exploit human vulnerabilities.

The Psychology of Social Engineering delves into the intricate art of manipulating human behaviour for nefarious purposes. Social engineers use various principles of persuasion, manipulation, and influence to exploit vulnerabilities in human psychology. Understanding these principles is crucial for defending against social engineering attacks.

Understanding these psychological principles helps individuals and organisations recognise and defend against social engineering tactics. By cultivating awareness and implementing robust security protocols, individuals can become less susceptible to manipulation and exploitation.

Key aspects of the psychology of social engineering includes:

1. **Principles of Persuasion**:

    - **Reciprocity**: People tend to feel obligated to return favours. Social engineers exploit this by providing something small or beneficial before making a request.

    - **Commitment and Consistency**: Once a person commits to something, they are more likely to follow through. Social engineers aim to get a small commitment before asking for a larger one.

    - **Social Proof**: People often look to others for guidance on how to behave, especially in uncertain situations. Social engineers create a sense of consensus or popularity around their requests.

    - **Authority**: People tend to follow figures of authority. Social engineers may impersonate authoritative figures or use props to appear legitimate.

    - **Liking**: People are more likely to comply with requests from those they like or find attractive. Social engineers employ charm, compliments, or other techniques to establish rapport.

2. **Manipulation Techniques**:
    - **Deception**: Social engineers often rely on deception, using false information, pretexting, or impersonation to gain trust or access.

    - **Tailgating**: This involves following an authorized person into a secure area, exploiting the natural tendency to be polite and hold doors open.

    - **Pretexting**: Social engineers create a fabricated scenario or pretext to manipulate the target into divulging information or performing an action.

    - **Quid Pro Quo**: Offering something in return for information or access, creating a perceived exchange of value.

3. **Influence Strategies**:
    - **Scarcity**: Creating a sense of urgency or scarcity can motivate quick decisions. Social engineers may claim limited availability or impending consequences.

    - **Emotional Manipulation**: Leveraging emotions like fear, greed, or sympathy to influence decision-making.

- **Appeal to Self-Interest**: Social engineers frame their requests in a way that aligns with the target's personal interests or goals.

4. **Exploiting Cognitive Biases**:
   - **Confirmation Bias**: People tend to seek information that confirms their pre-existing beliefs. Social engineers use this to reinforce their narratives.
   - **Authority Bias**: Placing undue trust in authoritative figures, even when they may not be legitimate.

5. **Creating a Sense of Urgency**:
   - Social engineers often create a false sense of urgency to pressure targets into making hasty decisions or divulging sensitive information.

What is the term Social Engineering?
- Social engineering refers to the psychological manipulation and deception techniques used by attackers to exploit human behaviour and gain unauthorised access to sensitive information, systems, or physical spaces. Instead of relying on technical vulnerabilities, social engineering exploits the innate human tendency to trust and respond to certain situations or requests.
- The goal of social engineering is to deceive individuals or manipulate them into performing actions that may compromise security, divulge confidential information, or provide unauthorised access.

Essentially, social engineering can be achieved through various tactics, including:
- **Impersonation:** The attacker poses as a trusted individual, such as a colleague, supervisor, or service provider, to gain the target's trust and manipulate them into providing sensitive information or performing specific actions.
- **Pretexting:** The attacker creates a fictional scenario or identity to establish credibility and manipulate the target. They may impersonate a customer, an IT technician, or a law enforcement officer, using persuasive tactics to convince the target to disclose confidential information or perform actions that benefit the attacker.
- **Phishing:** Phishing involves sending deceptive emails, messages, or communication to trick the target into revealing sensitive information, such as passwords, credit card details, or login credentials. These communications often mimic legitimate entities or urgent situations, exploiting the target's curiosity, fear, or desire for assistance.

- **Baiting:** Baiting involves enticing the target with a seemingly valuable or desirable item, such as a USB drive, CD, or a fake website, which contains malicious software or traps. The target unknowingly downloads malware or provides login credentials, compromising their security.

- **Tailgating:** In physical social engineering, the attacker gains unauthorised access to restricted areas by closely following an authorised individual through security checkpoints or doors. This tactic relies on the target's natural tendency to hold doors open or assume the attacker is authorised.

- Social engineering attacks can occur through various communication channels, including in-person interactions, phone calls, emails, or online messaging platforms. The success of social engineering attacks depends on the attacker's ability to exploit human psychology, manipulate emotions, create a sense of urgency, or establish trust.

- Mitigating social engineering attacks requires a combination of user awareness, education, and robust security measures. This includes training individuals to recognise and respond appropriately to suspicious requests, implementing strong authentication mechanisms, maintaining up-to-date security software, and establishing incident response protocols to address potential breaches resulting from social engineering tactics.

2.4.2 Common Social Engineering Techniques

This section provides a detailed exploration of common social engineering techniques, including phishing, pretexting, tailgating, and baiting. Readers will learn to recognise these tactics and implement countermeasures to protect against them.

Common Social Engineering Techniques and Tactics:

1. **Phishing:** Attackers send emails or messages disguised as legitimate organisations, asking recipients to click on malicious links or provide sensitive information.

    - **Countermeasure:** Employee training on recognising phishing emails and using email filtering systems to detect suspicious emails.

2. **Pretexting:** Attackers create a fabricated scenario to manipulate the target into providing sensitive information.

    - **Countermeasure:** Implementing strict verification processes for sensitive information requests and educating employees about verifying identities in unusual situations.

3. **Tailgating and Piggybacking:** Attackers gain physical access to restricted areas by following authorised personnel.

   - **Countermeasure:** Implementing access control measures like ID badges, security checkpoints, and enforcing a strict "no tailgating" policy.

4. **Baiting:** Attackers offer something enticing, like a USB drive or download link, which contains malicious software.

   - **Countermeasure:** Discouraging the use of external devices, regularly updating antivirus software, and educating employees about the risks of downloading from untrusted sources.

5. **Quid Pro Quo:** Attackers offer something in exchange for sensitive information.

   - **Countermeasure:** Educating employees about the importance of not disclosing sensitive information, and implementing policies against exchanging information for goods or services

2.4.3 Defending Against Social Engineering Attacks

Defending against social engineering requires a combination of awareness, education, and technical safeguards. This section offers practical advice and best practices for individuals and organisations to fortify themselves against social engineering attacks.

Implementing the following countermeasures fosters a security-conscious culture, organisations can significantly reduce the risk of falling victim to social engineering attacks. Cybersecurity is an ongoing effort, and staying vigilant is key to maintaining a robust defence against evolving threats.

1. **Employee Training and Awareness:**

   - Regularly conduct cybersecurity training sessions to educate employees about various social engineering techniques and how to recognise them.

2. **Strict Access Controls:**

   - Implement physical security measures to prevent unauthorized access to sensitive areas and require multi-factor authentication for digital access.

3. **Email Filtering and Authentication:**

   - Use email filtering systems to detect and quarantine phishing emails. Implement email authentication protocols like SPF, DKIM, and DMARC.

4. **Incident Response Plans:**

- Have a well-defined incident response plan in place to respond to social engineering incidents quickly and effectively.

5. **Endpoint Security:**
    - Use antivirus, anti-malware, and endpoint detection solutions to detect and mitigate malicious software.

6. **Data Classification and Handling:**
    - Clearly define and enforce policies for handling sensitive information, and limit access to authorised personnel.

7. **Security Culture:**
    - Foster a culture of security awareness, where employees feel comfortable reporting suspicious activity and understand the importance of security measures.

8. **Regular Security Audits and Assessments:**
    - Conduct regular security assessments to identify vulnerabilities and gaps in security measures.

Conclusion Tutorial Activity

These quizzes cover various aspects of malicious software, detecting and mitigating malware, and understanding social engineering, providing an opportunity for readers to test their knowledge:

Quiz 1: Understanding Malicious Software
1. What type of malicious software can replicate itself and spread to other files or systems?
2. How do worms differ from viruses in terms of spreading?
3. What is the primary purpose of Trojans?
4. Describe the impact of ransomware on victims.
5. What is the main function of spyware?
6. How do botnets operate?
7. Which type of malicious software displays unwanted advertisements?
8. Define the term "botnets."

Quiz 2: Detecting and Mitigating Malware
1. What are some practical strategies for identifying and neutralising malware?
2. List some reasons behind employing malicious software attacks.
3. How can regular backups help mitigate the impact of ransomware attacks?
4. What are some common impacts of diverse forms of malicious software on compromised systems?
5. Describe the case study of the CovidLock ransomware attack.
6. How do human factors contribute to enhancing the effectiveness of malicious software attacks?
7. What are some key steps in mitigating social engineering attacks?
8. Why is user awareness crucial in defending against social engineering attacks?

Quiz 3: Knowing About Social Engineering
1. Define social engineering.
2. List some common social engineering techniques and tactics.
3. How can organisations defend against social engineering attacks?
4. Explain the concept of pretexting.
5. What are some countermeasures against phishing attacks?
6. Describe the impact of social engineering attacks on organisations.
7. How can a security-conscious culture help mitigate social engineering risks?
8. Give an example of a social engineering technique involving physical access.

Chapter 3: Upholding Cybersecurity Governance and Compliance

Learning Outcome
- **3.1 Understand common types of testing in cyber security.**
    - Explain different types of cyber security testing.
    - Identify why cyber security testing is important.
    - Compare types of cyber security testing.
    - Consider mitigations following cyber security testing.
    - Explain why it is important to retest following any changes made.
    - Explain how the outcomes of cyber security testing can be reported.
    - Explain why the outcomes of cyber security testing must be reported.
- **3.2 Be able to reduce or remove potential cyber security vulnerabilities.**
    - Identify cyber security vulnerabilities.
    - Demonstrate the steps to be taken when a vulnerability has been identified.
    - Apply the correct response to the vulnerability.
    - Develop an appropriate communication to mitigate future vulnerabilities.
- **3.3 Understand controls in cyber security.**
    - Identify cyber security controls.
    - Explain a basic cyber security framework.
    - Evaluate a cyber security framework.
- **3.4 Be able to apply a cyber security control.**
    - Explain how to apply controls.
    - Implement a basic cyber security control.
    - Justify the implementation of the chosen cyber security control.
    - Explain why a control might not be applied.

3. About this chapter

Chapter 3 is a comprehensive exploration of the dynamic landscape of cybersecurity, focusing on testing methodologies, vulnerability management, and the implementation of crucial security controls. The chapter begins by dissecting various types of cybersecurity testing, elucidating the unique purposes and approaches of penetration testing, vulnerability scanning, security code review, and security configuration review. Emphasis is placed on the multifaceted nature of these assessments, each contributing to a holistic evaluation of an organisation's security posture.

The narrative seamlessly transitions to the significance of cybersecurity testing, underscoring its role in proactively identifying vulnerabilities, assessing overall security posture, meeting compliance requirements, and mitigating risks. The chapter provides a detailed comparison of different testing types, such as penetration testing versus vulnerability scanning and manual testing versus automated testing, offering readers a nuanced understanding of their strengths and limitations.

The subsequent sections delve into the critical steps that organisations must take after identifying vulnerabilities, including documentation, impact assessment, risk prioritisation, communication, remediation, testing, and continuous monitoring. This strategic approach provides a roadmap for organisations to systematically respond to and mitigate potential security threats.

Section 3.3 introduces readers to cybersecurity controls, essential mechanisms designed to safeguard systems, networks, and data. The discussion encompasses a spectrum of controls, including access controls, firewalls, intrusion detection/prevention systems, encryption, and incident response planning. A basic cybersecurity framework, exemplified by the NIST Cybersecurity Framework, is presented as a structured approach to managing and improving overall security posture.

The evaluation of a cybersecurity framework, covered in Section 3.3.3, guides readers in assessing the relevance, completeness, flexibility, scalability, and usability of such frameworks. Practical considerations such as integration with existing controls, compliance with industry standards, and ongoing support are highlighted to assist organisations in choosing the most suitable framework for their specific needs.

In Section 3.4, the focus shifts to the practical application of cybersecurity controls. The chapter outlines a systematic approach for organisations to follow, from identifying relevant controls based on specific security requirements to testing and validating their effectiveness. The implementation of a basic cybersecurity control, exemplified by strong password policies, is detailed, accompanied by justifications for its adoption.

Concluding the chapter, the discussion turns to reasons why a cybersecurity control might not be applied, emphasizing factors such as infeasibility, cost-benefit analysis, business impact, legal or regulatory constraints, and strategic risk acceptance or transfer.

In essence, Chapter 3 serves as an indispensable guide for readers, offering a holistic understanding of cybersecurity testing methodologies, vulnerability management strategies, and the implementation of controls to fortify digital defences in an ever-evolving threat landscape. The chapter includes quizzes in each section to help reinforce key concepts and understanding of cybersecurity governance and compliance.

3.1.1: Understand Common Types of Testing in Cybersecurity

Cybersecurity testing is a multi-faceted approach to assessing the security posture of an organisation's systems, networks, and applications. There are several distinct types of cybersecurity testing, each with its unique focus and purpose. Some common types include:

Penetration Testing:

Penetration testing, also known as ethical hacking, involves simulating real-world cyberattacks on a system or network to identify vulnerabilities. This assessment helps to evaluate the effectiveness of security measures and pinpoint potential points of exploitation.

Vulnerability Scanning:

This method employs automated tools to scan a system or network for known vulnerabilities. It provides a quick overview of potential weaknesses but doesn't involve active exploitation like penetration testing.

Security Code Review:

This type of testing involves analysing the source code of an application or software to identify any security flaws or vulnerabilities. It uncovers issues that may not be evident during other types of testing.

Security Configuration Review:

This testing focuses on reviewing the configuration settings of systems, networks, and applications to ensure they are properly configured and comply with security best practices. It helps identify misconfigurations that could lead to security breaches.

Security Awareness Training:

While not a traditional testing method, security awareness training plays a crucial role in educating employees about cyber threats, safe practices, and how to recognise and report suspicious activities. It strengthens the human element of security.

Quiz: Types of Cybersecurity Testing
1. What type of cybersecurity testing involves simulating real-world cyberattacks to identify vulnerabilities?
2. Which testing method employs automated tools to scan systems or networks for known vulnerabilities?
3. Which testing type involves analysing the source code of an application or software for security flaws?
4. What type of testing focuses on reviewing the configuration settings of systems, networks, and applications?
5. Though not a traditional testing method, what plays a crucial role in educating employees about cyber threats?

3.1.2 Identify Why Cybersecurity Testing Is Important

Cybersecurity testing holds significant importance for several reasons:

Identify Vulnerabilities:

Testing helps uncover weaknesses, vulnerabilities, and potential points of exploitation in systems, networks, and applications. This allows organizations to proactively address these issues before they can be exploited by malicious actors.

Assess Security Posture:

Testing provides an evaluation of an organization's overall security posture. It helps determine if existing security controls and measures are effective and identify areas that require improvement.

Compliance Requirements:

Many industries and regulatory frameworks require regular security testing to ensure compliance with specific standards and regulations. Testing helps demonstrate due diligence in protecting sensitive data and maintaining regulatory compliance.

Risk Mitigation:

By identifying vulnerabilities and weaknesses, testing allows organizations to prioritize and mitigate risks. It helps allocate resources effectively to address the most critical security issues and reduce the likelihood of successful cyber-attacks.

Continuous Improvement:

Cybersecurity testing is an iterative process that promotes continuous improvement. Regular testing and retesting help organizations stay vigilant against evolving threats and adapt their security measures accordingly.

Quiz: Importance of Cybersecurity Testing
1. Why is cybersecurity testing important in identifying vulnerabilities?
2. What does cybersecurity testing assess regarding an organisation's overall security posture?
3. What role does cybersecurity testing play in complying with industry standards and regulations?
4. How does cybersecurity testing contribute to risk mitigation?
5. Why is cybersecurity testing considered an iterative process?

3.1.3 Compare Types of Cybersecurity Testing

Different types of cybersecurity testing have distinct approaches and objectives. Here's a comparison of some common testing types:

Penetration Testing vs. Vulnerability Scanning:
- **Penetration Testing:** Involves simulating real-world attacks to identify vulnerabilities through active exploitation. It provides a more comprehensive assessment but requires skilled testers.

- **Vulnerability Scanning:** Uses automated tools to identify known vulnerabilities but doesn't involve active exploitation.

Security Code Review vs. Security Configuration Review:
- **Security Code Review:** Involves analysing the source code to identify security flaws. It is typically performed by experienced developers or security specialists.
- **Security Configuration Review:** Focuses on assessing the configuration settings of systems, networks, and applications.

Internal Testing vs. External Testing:
- **Internal Testing:** Performed from within the organization's network, simulating attacks by insiders or compromised systems.
- **External Testing:** Involves assessing the security of systems and networks from an external perspective, simulating attacks from outside sources.

Manual Testing vs. Automated Testing:
- **Manual Testing:** Involves skilled testers manually assessing systems and applications for vulnerabilities. It allows for greater flexibility and depth but can be time-consuming.
- **Automated Testing:** Relies on software tools to identify vulnerabilities and weaknesses more efficiently but may not capture all possible issues.

Quiz: Comparison of Cybersecurity Testing
1. How does penetration testing differ from vulnerability scanning?
2. What distinguishes security code review from security configuration review?
3. What's the main difference between internal testing and external testing?
4. Define the contrast between manual testing and automated testing.

3.1.4 Consider Mitigations Following Cybersecurity Testing

After conducting cybersecurity testing, organizations should implement mitigations to address identified vulnerabilities and weaknesses. Some common steps include:

Patching and Updating:

Apply necessary security patches and updates to software, systems, and network devices to address known vulnerabilities.

Configuration Adjustments:

Review and adjust configuration settings to ensure compliance with security best practices. This may involve disabling unnecessary services, implementing secure communication protocols, and enabling proper access controls.

Network Segmentation:

Implement network segmentation to isolate critical systems and limit the potential impact of a security breach.

Access Controls and Authentication:

Strengthen access controls by implementing strong authentication mechanisms such as multi-factor authentication (MFA) and role-based access control (RBAC).

Security Awareness Training:

Provide ongoing security awareness training to employees to educate them about the latest threats, safe practices, and how to report security incidents.

Incident Response Planning:

Develop and maintain an effective incident response plan to ensure a timely and coordinated response to security incidents.

Quiz: Mitigations Following Cybersecurity Testing

1. What steps should organisations take concerning patching and updating after cybersecurity testing?
2. What adjustments might organisations make in terms of security configuration after testing?
3. What purpose does network segmentation serve as a mitigation strategy?
4. How can access controls and authentication be strengthened following cybersecurity testing?
5. What role does security awareness training play in mitigating cybersecurity risks?

3.1.5 Why Is It Important to Retest Following Any Changes Made

Retesting following any changes is essential for the following reasons:

Verification of Effectiveness:

Retesting ensures that the implemented changes have effectively addressed the identified vulnerabilities or weaknesses. It provides assurance that the security measures put in place are working as intended.

Unintended Consequences:

Changes made to systems, applications, or configurations can have unintended consequences, such as introducing new vulnerabilities or affecting the functionality of the system. Retesting helps identify any unintended consequences and allows for timely remediation.

Changing Threat Landscape:

The threat landscape is dynamic, with new vulnerabilities and attack techniques emerging regularly. Retesting helps ensure that systems and applications remain resilient against evolving threats.

Compliance Requirements:

Many compliance frameworks and regulations require periodic retesting after changes are made to systems or applications. Retesting helps demonstrate ongoing compliance and due diligence.

Quiz: Importance of Retesting
1. Why is retesting essential following any changes made after cybersecurity testing?
2. What are some potential unintended consequences of changes made to systems or applications?
3. How does retesting help ensure resilience against evolving threats?
4. Name one reason why compliance frameworks and regulations require periodic retesting after changes are made.

3.1.6 How the Outcomes of Cybersecurity Testing Can Be Reported

The outcomes of cybersecurity testing can be reported in various formats, depending on the intended audience and purpose. Below are some common reporting methods:

Test Reports:

Detailed reports that document the testing methodology, objectives, findings, and recommendations. They provide comprehensive information for technical stakeholders, such as IT teams and security professionals.

Executive Summaries:

Summarized reports tailored for non-technical stakeholders, such as senior management or board members. They focus on high-level findings, risks, and recommendations in a concise and easily understandable format.

Dashboards and Metrics:

Visual representations, such as dashboards or scorecards, that highlight key metrics, vulnerabilities, and their severity levels. They provide a quick overview of the security posture and progress over time.

Remediation Plans:

Action plans that outline the steps needed to address identified vulnerabilities and weaknesses. They prioritise remediation efforts and provide a roadmap for improving security.

Presentations and Meetings:

Oral presentations or meetings with stakeholders to discuss the findings, recommendations, and any necessary clarifications. These interactions allow for direct engagement, question-and-answer sessions, and further discussion of the test results.

3.1.7 Why Outcomes Must Be Reported:

- **Awareness:** Reporting increases awareness of the security risks and vulnerabilities that exist within an organization's systems, networks, and applications.

- **Decision-making:** The outcomes of testing provide valuable information for decision-making. Stakeholders can prioritise and allocate resources to address identified vulnerabilities based on severity.

- **Accountability:** Reporting helps establish accountability for the security of an organization

- **Compliance:** Reporting is often required to demonstrate compliance with industry regulations, legal requirements, and contractual obligations.

- **Continuous Improvement:** Reporting allows organizations to track their progress in addressing vulnerabilities over time.

Quiz: Reporting Outcomes of Cybersecurity Testing
1. What are test reports in the context of cybersecurity testing?
2. Who are executive summaries tailored for in cybersecurity testing reporting?
3. How do dashboards and metrics help in reporting cybersecurity testing outcomes?
4. What information do remediation plans typically include?
5. Why are oral presentations or meetings conducted to discuss cybersecurity testing outcomes?

3.2 Reduce or Remove Potential Cybersecurity Vulnerability
3.2.1 Identify Cybersecurity Vulnerabilities

Identifying cybersecurity vulnerabilities involves assessing systems, cloud-based, on-premises networks, and applications to uncover weaknesses that could be exploited by attackers. Some common methods for identifying vulnerabilities include:

Vulnerability Scanning:

Using automated tools to scan systems and networks for known vulnerabilities. These tools compare the current software versions and configurations against a database of known vulnerabilities to identify potential weaknesses.

Penetration Testing:

Conducting controlled attacks on systems and networks to simulate real-world scenarios and identify vulnerabilities. Penetration testers attempt to exploit security weaknesses to gain unauthorized access or perform malicious actions.

Security Code Review:

Analysing the source code of applications or software to identify coding errors, insecure practices, or vulnerabilities. This manual review helps uncover vulnerabilities that might not be apparent through other testing methods.

Security Configuration Review:

Assessing the configuration settings of systems, networks, and applications to identify misconfigurations or insecure settings that could lead to vulnerabilities.

Quiz: Identifying Cybersecurity Vulnerabilities
1. What is vulnerability scanning in the context of cybersecurity?
2. How does penetration testing differ from vulnerability scanning?
3. What is the main goal of security code review in identifying vulnerabilities?
4. Describe the process of security configuration review.
5. Which method of identifying vulnerabilities involves automated tools comparing software versions against a database of known vulnerabilities?

3.2.2 Demonstrate the Steps to Be Taken When a Vulnerability Has Been Identified

When a vulnerability has been identified, the following seven (7) steps should be taken:

Document the Vulnerability:

Accurately document and record the details of the vulnerability. Include information such as the system or application affected, the nature of the vulnerability, its severity, and any supporting evidence or test results.

Assess the Impact:

Determine the potential impact of the vulnerability on the confidentiality, integrity, and availability of the system or data. Evaluate the severity of the vulnerability based on its potential consequences.

Prioritise and Assign Risk Levels:

Prioritise vulnerabilities based on their severity and potential impact. Assign risk levels (e.g., low, medium, high) to help prioritize remediation efforts.

Communicate the Findings:

Notify relevant stakeholders, such as system owners, IT teams, or security personnel, about the identified vulnerability. Provide clear and concise information about the vulnerability, its potential impact, and any recommended actions.

Remediate the Vulnerability:

Develop a plan to address the vulnerability and mitigate the risk. This may involve applying security patches, updating software versions, changing configurations, or implementing additional security controls.

Test the Remediation:

After applying the necessary fixes or mitigations, retest the system or application to ensure that the vulnerability has been effectively addressed. Verify that the remediation actions have resolved the vulnerability without introducing any unintended consequences.

Monitor and Review:

Continuously monitor the system or application for any recurring vulnerabilities or new threats. Regularly review security measures, configurations, and processes to prevent similar vulnerabilities from reoccurring.

Quiz: Steps to Be Taken When a Vulnerability Is Identified
1. Why is it important to accurately document and record details of a vulnerability?
2. What factors should be considered when assessing the impact of a vulnerability?
3. How can vulnerabilities be prioritized and assigned risk levels?
4. Who should be notified about the identified vulnerability?
5. What are some common methods for remediating vulnerabilities?
6. Why is it necessary to test the remediation after applying fixes or mitigations?
7. What is the importance of continuously monitoring and reviewing systems after addressing vulnerabilities?

3.2.3 Apply the Correct Response to the Vulnerability

The response to a vulnerability will depend on its severity, potential impact, and the specific context of the affected system or application. Some general response options include:

Apply Security Patch:

If a vendor-supplied security patch is available, apply it to address the vulnerability. Patches often contain fixes that mitigate or eliminate the vulnerability.

Update Software Versions:

Update software versions to the latest stable release, as newer versions may include security enhancements and bug fixes.

Change Configurations:

Modify system or application configurations to eliminate or reduce the vulnerability. This may involve disabling unnecessary services, enabling security features, or implementing access controls.

Implement Additional Security Controls:

Deploy additional security measures, such as firewalls, intrusion detection systems (IDS), or access control mechanisms, to mitigate the vulnerability and protect against potential exploits.

Develop and Apply Workarounds:

If an immediate fix is not available, implement temporary workarounds to reduce the vulnerability's risk. Workarounds may involve modifying configurations, restricting access, or implementing compensating controls.

Conduct Security Awareness Training:

Educate users and employees about the vulnerability, its potential impact, and safe practices to mitigate the risk. Raise awareness of the importance of following security policies and reporting any suspicious activities.

Quiz: Applying the Correct Response to Vulnerabilities

1. What factors determine the appropriate response to a cybersecurity vulnerability?
2. How does applying a security patch help address vulnerabilities?
3. Why is it important to update software versions to the latest stable release?
4. Give examples of configuration changes that can help mitigate vulnerabilities.
5. What are some additional security controls that can be implemented to mitigate vulnerabilities?
6. When might it be necessary to develop and apply workarounds for vulnerabilities?
7. How does security awareness training contribute to mitigating vulnerabilities?

3.2.4 Develop an Appropriate Communication to Mitigate Future Vulnerabilities

To mitigate future vulnerabilities, effective communication via email, newsletter, or leaflet is crucial. Some key considerations for developing appropriate communications include:

Clear and Concise:

Ensure that the communication is easy to understand, avoiding technical jargon whenever possible. Use plain language to explain the vulnerability, its potential impact, and the recommended actions in a clear and concise manner.

Targeted Audience:

Tailor the communication to the specific audience, considering their technical expertise and roles. Provide the necessary information for each audience to understand the vulnerability and its implications.

Actionable Recommendations:

Include specific and actionable recommendations for mitigating the vulnerability. Provide step-by-step instructions or links to relevant resources that can help users or system owners implement the necessary changes.

Timely Delivery:

Communicate the vulnerability promptly, especially if it poses a significant risk. Timely delivery allows stakeholders to take immediate action to mitigate the vulnerability.

Follow-up and Updates:

Provide regular updates on the status of the vulnerability, including progress on remediation efforts and any changes in the risk level. Keep stakeholders informed of any new developments or recommended actions as they arise.

Training and Awareness:

Incorporate security awareness training into the communication to educate stakeholders on safe practices, potential indicators of compromise, and how to report suspicious activities. Reinforce the importance of maintaining a proactive security posture.

Lessons Learned:

Use the communication as an opportunity to share lessons learned from the vulnerability. Highlight any underlying causes, systemic issues, or best practices that can help prevent similar vulnerabilities in the future.

By developing effective communications via emails, newsletters, or leaflets, organisations can raise awareness, promote accountability, and foster a culture of security awareness to mitigate future vulnerabilities.

Quiz: Develop an Appropriate Communication to Mitigate Future Vulnerabilities

1. Why is clear and concise communication important when addressing vulnerabilities?
2. How should communication be tailored in terms of the audience?
3. What should actionable recommendations in vulnerability communications entail?
4. Why is timely delivery of vulnerability communication crucial?
5. What role does follow-up and updates play in vulnerability communication?
6. How can training and awareness be integrated into vulnerability communication?
7. Why is it valuable to share lessons learned in vulnerability communications?

3.3 Understand Controls in Cybersecurity
3.3.1 Identify Cybersecurity Controls

Cybersecurity controls are critical measures and mechanisms put in place to safeguard systems, networks, and data from cyber threats. They are designed to prevent, detect, and respond to security incidents. The common cybersecurity controls include:

Access Controls:

Ensure that only authorised individuals can access resources or perform specific actions. This includes mechanisms like strong authentication, access control lists, and user permissions.

Firewalls:

Act as a barrier between internal and external networks, monitoring and controlling incoming and outgoing network traffic based on predetermined security rules.

Intrusion Detection and Prevention Systems (IDS/IPS):

Monitor network traffic for suspicious or malicious activities and take proactive measures to prevent or mitigate potential attacks.

Encryption:

Protect sensitive data by converting it into a form that can only be accessed with the correct decryption key. Encryption can be applied to data at rest, in transit, or in use.

Patch Management:

Regularly apply security patches and updates to software, operating systems, and applications to address known vulnerabilities.

Security Information and Event Management (SIEM):

Collect, analyse, and correlate security event logs from various sources to identify and respond to potential security incidents.

Security Awareness Training:

Educate users and employees about potential cyber threats, safe practices, and how to recognise and report security incidents.

Incident Response Planning:

Develop and maintain a documented plan that outlines the steps to be taken in the event of a security incident, including incident detection, containment, eradication, and recovery.

Backup and Disaster Recovery:

Regularly back up critical data and systems and establish procedures for recovering and restoring them in the event of a security incident or system failure.

Physical Security Controls:

Implement physical measures, such as access controls, surveillance systems, and secure facilities, to protect physical assets and prevent unauthorised access.

Quiz: Understand Controls in Cybersecurity
1. What are cybersecurity controls, and why are they important?
2. Explain the purpose of access controls in cybersecurity.
3. How do firewalls contribute to cybersecurity?
4. What is the role of Intrusion Detection and Prevention Systems (IDS/IPS) in cybersecurity?
5. Define encryption and its significance in cybersecurity.
6. Why is patch management essential in cybersecurity?
7. What is the function of Security Information and Event Management (SIEM) systems?

8. How does security awareness training contribute to cybersecurity?
9. Describe the purpose of incident response planning in cybersecurity.
10. Why are backup and disaster recovery procedures critical in cybersecurity?

3.3.2 Basic Cybersecurity Framework

A basic cybersecurity framework provides a structured approach to managing and improving an organisation's overall security posture. It aligns security objectives with business goals, identifies, and prioritises risks, and establishes a framework for implementing security controls. One widely recognised framework is the NIST Cybersecurity Framework (National Institute of Standards and Technology). It consists of standards, guidelines, and best practices organised into the following key components:

Identify:

Identify and understand the assets, systems, data, and capabilities that need to be protected. Conduct risk assessments and prioritise critical assets.

Protect:

Implement safeguards to protect against potential cyber threats. This includes access controls, secure configurations, data encryption, security awareness training, and implementing appropriate security controls.

Detect:

Implement measures to detect and identify security incidents promptly. This includes implementing monitoring systems, intrusion detection systems, log analysis, and security event monitoring.

Respond:

Develop an incident response plan to respond effectively to security incidents. Establish procedures for containment, eradication, recovery, and communication during a security incident.

Recover:

Establish processes and mechanisms for recovering from a security incident. This includes backup and restoration procedures, system and data recovery, and learning from incidents to improve resilience.

Continuous Improvement:

Continuously assess and improve the effectiveness of security controls and practices. Regularly review and update policies, conduct security audits, and stay informed about emerging threats and best practices.

Quiz: Basic Cybersecurity Framework
1. What is the purpose of a basic cybersecurity framework?
2. What does the "Identify" component of the NIST Cybersecurity Framework involve?
3. Provide examples of safeguards implemented in the "Protect" component of the NIST Cybersecurity Framework.
4. How does the "Detect" component of the NIST Framework contribute to cybersecurity?
5. What are the key elements of an incident response plan as outlined in the "Respond" component of the NIST Framework?
6. Explain the importance of the "Recover" component in cybersecurity.
7. How does continuous improvement play a role in maintaining cybersecurity according to the NIST Framework?
8. Why is it essential for organisations to prioritise critical assets in the cybersecurity framework?
9. Describe the role of security awareness training in the protection of an organisation's assets.
10. How do security audits contribute to continuous improvement in cybersecurity frameworks?

3.3.3 Evaluate a Cybersecurity Framework

When evaluating a cybersecurity framework, consider the following factors:

Relevance:

Determine if the framework aligns with your organisation's industry, regulatory requirements, and specific security needs. Assess if it provides guidance and controls that address the unique risks and challenges your organisation faces.

Completeness:

Evaluate the framework's coverage of key areas such as risk management, governance, technical controls, incident response, and continuous improvement. Ensure that all critical aspects of security are addressed.

Flexibility and Scalability:

Assess whether the framework can be tailored to your organisation's size, complexity, and growth. It should be adaptable to accommodate changes in technology, evolving threats, and business requirements.

Integration:

Consider how the framework aligns with existing security controls, processes, and frameworks in your organisation. Evaluate if it can be integrated with other frameworks or standards that you follow, such as ISO 27001 or COBIT.

Usability:

Assess the framework's clarity, usability, and practicality. Evaluate if it provides actionable guidance, templates, and resources that can be readily implemented. It should be understandable and accessible to stakeholders at different levels of technical expertise.

Maturity:

Consider the maturity and acceptance of the framework within the industry. Look for case studies, success stories, and feedback from organisations that have implemented the framework.

Compliance and Assurance:

Evaluate if the framework supports compliance with relevant regulations, standards, and best practices. Consider if it provides mechanisms for measuring and demonstrating compliance, and if it facilitates security audits or assessments.

Updates and Support:

Investigate whether the framework is actively maintained and updated to address emerging threats and changing security landscapes. Determine if there is a support community, resources, and guidance available for implementation and ongoing support.

Example:

If an organisation chooses not to encrypt network traffic, it has both advantages and disadvantages. By carefully considering these advantages and disadvantages, organisations can make informed decisions about whether to implement encryption for their network traffic.

Advantages:
1. **Network Performance:** Encryption and decryption processes add overhead to network traffic, potentially impacting network speeds and latency. By not encrypting the traffic, the organisation may achieve higher network performance.

2. **Simplified Monitoring:** Without encryption, network administrators can easily monitor and inspect network traffic for troubleshooting, performance analysis, and security purposes. This allows for better identification of potential issues and detection of malicious activities.

3. **Faster Response Times:** With unencrypted traffic, organisations can quickly analyse and respond to network incidents, such as identifying and mitigating security threats, as they have clear visibility into the content of the traffic.

4. **Cost Savings:** Implementing encryption requires additional hardware, software, and configuration, which can be expensive. By not implementing encryption, organisations can save costs associated with encryption systems.

Disadvantages:
1. **Data Privacy and Security:** Unencrypted network traffic is susceptible to eavesdropping and interception by malicious actors, leading to unauthorised access to sensitive information. Encryption helps protect the confidentiality and integrity of data during transit.

2. **Regulatory Compliance:** Many industries have strict regulations regarding data privacy and security. Not encrypting network traffic can result in non-compliance, potentially leading to legal and financial consequences.

3. **Data Breaches and Reputational Damage:** Intercepted sensitive data due to lack of encryption can lead to data breaches and significant reputational damage for the organisation. Customers and partners may lose trust in the organisation's ability to protect their data.

4. **Insider Threats:** Without encryption, insider threats within the organisation have easier access to sensitive information transmitted over the network. Encryption can help mitigate the risk of unauthorised access and data leakage by limiting the ability of insiders to interpret the intercepted traffic.

5. **Compliance with Partners' Requirements:** Organisations that exchange data with partners or clients who require encrypted communication may face challenges if

they do not implement encryption. It can hinder business collaborations and partnerships.

Quiz: Evaluate a Cybersecurity Framework
1. What factors should be considered when evaluating a cybersecurity framework?
2. Explain the importance of relevance in the evaluation of a cybersecurity framework.
3. What does completeness refer to in the context of cybersecurity frameworks?
4. How does flexibility and scalability contribute to the effectiveness of a cybersecurity framework?
5. Describe the significance of integration when evaluating a cybersecurity framework.
6. What aspects of usability should be assessed during the evaluation of a cybersecurity framework?
7. Why is the maturity of a cybersecurity framework important in the evaluation process?
8. How does compliance and assurance factor into the evaluation of cybersecurity frameworks?
9. Discuss the importance of updates and support in maintaining a cybersecurity framework's effectiveness.
10. Provide an example of a scenario where an organisation chooses not to encrypt network traffic and list advantages and disadvantages of this decision.

3.4 Applying Cybersecurity Controls
3.4.1 How to apply cybersecurity controls.

To apply cybersecurity controls effectively, follow these steps:
1. **Identify Relevant Controls:** Based on the specific security requirements and risks of your organisation, identify the controls that are most appropriate and relevant. Consider industry best practices, regulatory requirements, and the nature of your systems, networks, and data.

2. **Assess Control Suitability:** Evaluate the suitability of each control for your organisation's context. Consider factors such as feasibility, cost, resources, and compatibility with existing systems and processes.

3. **Develop Implementation Plan:** Create a detailed plan that outlines the steps, resources, and timeline required to implement the controls. Assign responsibilities to individuals or teams for executing specific tasks.

4. **Allocate Resources:** Ensure that you have the necessary resources, including personnel, budget, and tools, to implement the controls effectively. Allocate resources based on the priority and criticality of each control.

5. **Implement Controls:** Follow the implementation plan and execute the necessary actions to deploy the controls. This may involve configuring security settings, deploying hardware or software solutions, developing policies and procedures, or conducting security awareness training.

6. **Test and Validate:** Once the controls are implemented, test and validate their effectiveness. Conduct assessments, penetration tests, or vulnerability scans to ensure that the controls are functioning as intended and providing the desired level of security.

7. **Monitor and Maintain:** Regularly monitor the implemented controls to ensure their ongoing effectiveness. Monitor for security incidents, conduct regular audits or assessments, and keep the controls up to date with patches and updates.

8. **Review and Improve:** Continuously review the effectiveness of the controls and identify areas for improvement. Seek feedback from stakeholders, monitor emerging threats, and update the controls as needed to address new risks and vulnerabilities.

3.4.2 Implement a basic cybersecurity control.

One example of implementing a basic cybersecurity control is implementing strong password policies. The steps to implement this control are:

1. **Define Password Requirements:** Determine the requirements for strong passwords based on industry best practices. This may include a minimum length, a combination of uppercase and lowercase letters, numbers, and special characters.

2. **Communicate the Policy:** Clearly communicate the password policy to all users and employees. Provide guidelines and instructions on creating and maintaining strong passwords.

3. **Enforce Password Changes:** Implement a policy that requires regular password changes to mitigate the risk of compromised passwords. Define a suitable time interval for password expiration and communicate it to users.

4. **Implement Password Complexity Rules:** Configure systems and applications to enforce the defined password requirements. Ensure that users are prompted to create strong passwords that meet the specified criteria.

5. **Educate Users:** Conduct security awareness training to educate users on the importance of strong passwords and the risks associated with weak or easily guessable passwords. Provide tips on creating memorable yet complex passwords, e.g., 'Patrick' becomes: #P4t3!q@

6. **Multi-Factor Authentication (MFA):** Consider implementing multi-factor authentication where possible. MFA adds an extra layer of security by requiring users to provide additional authentication factors, such as a code from a mobile app or a biometric scan, in addition to a password.

7. **Regular Auditing and Enforcement:** Periodically audit user passwords to identify weak or compromised passwords. Enforce password changes and educate users on best practices if weak passwords are identified.

3.4.3 Justify the implementation of the chosen cybersecurity control.

Implementing for example, strong password policies can be justified for several reasons:

- **Password Security:** Strong passwords make it more difficult for attackers to guess or crack passwords, thereby protecting user accounts and systems from unauthorised access.

- **Data Protection:** Strong passwords help protect sensitive data, including personal information, financial data, and intellectual property, from being compromised in the event of a security breach.

- **Compliance Requirements:** Many regulatory frameworks and industry standards require the implementation of strong password policies to safeguard customer data.

- **User Accountability:** By implementing strong password policies, organisations promote user accountability for protecting their accounts and data. It establishes a culture of security awareness and encourages responsible password management practices.

- **Risk Mitigation:** Weak or easily guessable passwords are a significant security risk. Implementing strong password policies helps mitigate this risk and strengthens the overall security posture of the organisation.

3.4.4 Why a cybersecurity control might not be applied.

There can be several reasons why a cybersecurity control might not be applied, for example, when is doing nothing a better option?

- **Infeasibility:** Some controls may be technically or operationally infeasible to implement due to compatibility issues, resource constraints, or limitations of existing systems or infrastructure. In such cases, alternative controls or mitigating measures should be considered.

- **Cost-Benefit Analysis:** The cost of implementing and maintaining a control may outweigh the potential benefits or the level of risk associated with the threat. Organisations need to evaluate the cost-effectiveness of controls and prioritise their implementation based on risk assessment.

- **Business Impact:** Certain controls may have a significant impact on business operations, productivity, or user experience. In such cases, organisations may need to strike a balance between security requirements and operational efficiency.

- **Legal or Regulatory Constraints:** Certain controls may conflict with legal or regulatory requirements specific to an industry or jurisdiction. Organisations must ensure that controls align with applicable laws and regulations.

- **Risk Acceptance or Transfer:** In some cases, organisations may consciously choose to accept or transfer the risk associated with a control rather than implementing it directly. Risk acceptance may occur when the potential impact is low, the control is not feasible, or alternative risk mitigation strategies are in place.

Quiz: Applying Cybersecurity Controls

These quiz questions should help reinforce key concepts and understanding of cybersecurity controls and their implementation:

1. Why is it important to identify relevant controls based on the specific security requirements and risks of your organisation?

2. What factors should be considered when assessing the suitability of a cybersecurity control for an organisation's context?

3. Why is it necessary to create a detailed plan for implementing cybersecurity controls? Provide at least two reasons.

4. Describe why it's crucial to allocate resources based on the priority and criticality of each control during implementation.

5. What are some actions involved in deploying cybersecurity controls within an organisation?
6. Explain the importance of testing and validating implemented controls in cybersecurity.
7. What are some activities involved in regularly monitoring implemented cybersecurity controls?
8. Why is it essential to continuously review the effectiveness of cybersecurity controls and identify areas for improvement?
9. Outline the steps involved in implementing strong password policies within an organisation.
10. Provide at least three reasons why implementing strong password policies is justified within an organisation.
11. Enumerate three reasons why a cybersecurity control might not be applied within an organisation.

Chapter 4: Managing Cybersecurity Operations

Learning Outcome
- **4.1 Understand what is meant by a cybersecurity incident response plan.**
    - Describe what a cyber security incident response plan is used for.
    - Explain when a cyber security incident response plan is used.
    - Describe the stages of a cyber security incident response lifecycle.
- **4.2 Be able to develop a cybersecurity incident response plan.**
    - Explain why it is important to maintain an up-to-date cyber security incident log.
    - Explain the steps to be included within a cyber security incident response plan.
    - Explain why it is important to have a cyber security incident response plan.
    - Develop a cyber security incident response plan for an organisation.
- **4.3 Be able to develop an incident post-mortem report.**
    - Explain what is meant by incident postmortem.
    - Explain the structure of an incident postmortem.
    - Consider the importance of the following when carrying out an incident postmortem: • integrity • rigour • discipline.
    - Create a postmortem report of an incident.
    - Reflect upon the report and make recommendations based on the findings.
- **4.4 Integrating SMART objectives and SWOT analysis into cybersecurity incident response plan.**
    - The development and analysis of SMART objectives and SWOT analysis into the Cybersecurity Incident Response Plan

4. About this chapter

Chapter 4 of this book provides a comprehensive exploration of Cybersecurity Incident Response, a critical facet in the contemporary landscape of digital security. The chapter unfolds with a detailed exposition of a Cybersecurity Incident Response Plan (CIRP), highlighting its pivotal role as a structured framework when responding to cybersecurity incidents. This plan acts as a strategic guide, delineating the roles and responsibilities of the incident response team, communication protocols, and the necessary technical measures at each stage of the incident response process.

The tutorial activities within this chapter delve into the intricacies of cybersecurity incident response. They elucidate the activation of incident response plans when organisations face cybersecurity incidents, ranging from unauthorised access to denial-of-service attacks. The chapter then systematically walks through the stages of the cybersecurity incident response lifecycle, offering a comprehensive approach to incident management, from proactive preparation to post-incident activities.

Moving forward, the chapter sheds light on the crucial aspect of reducing or removing potential cybersecurity vulnerabilities. It emphasizes the importance of maintaining an up-to-date incident log, serving as a repository for incident details, trends analysis, compliance adherence, and continuous improvement of incident response processes.

The chapter concludes by delving into the development of an incident post-mortem report, elucidating its structure, and underscoring the significance of integrity, rigour, and discipline in the post-mortem process. A practical example in the form of a post-mortem report for a cybersecurity breach adds real-world context.

In the final section, readers are guided through reflecting upon the post-mortem report and making actionable recommendations based on the findings. These recommendations span various domains, including vulnerability management, employee training, incident response coordination, network segmentation, monitoring capabilities, security assessments, incident response testing, communication protocols, incident logging, and establishing a lesson learned repository.

In essence, Chapter 4 equips readers with the knowledge and tools needed to navigate the complex landscape of cybersecurity incidents. It emphasizes a proactive approach, structured response frameworks, and continuous improvement to fortify organisational resilience against evolving cyber threats. Uses of SMART objectives and SWOT analysis in CIRP are also highlighted.

4.1. Understanding Cybersecurity Incident Response Plan (CIRP)

The Cybersecurity Incident Response Plan (CIRP) is a crucial component of an organisation's overall cybersecurity strategy. It outlines the procedures and protocols to follow when a security incident occurs, aiming to minimise the impact on the organisation and facilitate a swift and effective response. By implementing a comprehensive Cybersecurity Incident Response Plan, organisations can effectively detect, respond to, and recover from security incidents, thereby minimising the impact on operations, reputation, and stakeholder trust. Some of the key aspects typically covered in a CIRP include:

1. **Incident Identification and Classification:** Define criteria for identifying and classifying security incidents based on severity, impact, and type. Establish clear indicators of compromise (IOCs) and anomalous behaviour to help detect potential incidents early.

2. **Response Team Roles and Responsibilities:** Clearly define the roles and responsibilities of individuals and teams involved in incident response. This may include members from IT, security, legal, communications, human resources, and executive management. Ensure that each team member understands their duties and escalation procedures.

3. **Communication Protocols:** Establish communication protocols for reporting, escalating, and disseminating information about security incidents. Define channels for internal communication within the response team, as well as external communication with stakeholders, partners, customers, regulatory bodies, and law enforcement agencies.

4. **Incident Containment and Mitigation:** Define procedures for containing and mitigating security incidents to prevent further damage and limit the scope of the incident. This may involve isolating affected systems, blocking malicious traffic, applying patches or updates, and implementing temporary security controls.

5. **Forensic Investigation and Evidence Preservation:** Outline procedures for conducting forensic investigations to determine the root cause of the incident, identify compromised systems or data, and gather evidence for potential legal or regulatory purposes. Ensure that forensic analysis is conducted in a manner that preserves the integrity and admissibility of evidence.

6. **Incident Recovery and Restoration:** Define steps for restoring affected systems and services to normal operation following a security incident. Develop recovery procedures for data restoration, system reconfiguration, and business continuity measures to minimise downtime and service disruptions.

7. **Post-Incident Analysis and Lessons Learned**: Establish processes for conducting post-incident analysis and lessons learned sessions to identify gaps, weaknesses, and areas for improvement in the incident response plan and overall cybersecurity posture. Document key findings and recommendations for enhancing incident detection, response, and prevention capabilities.

8. **Training and Awareness Programs**: Provide regular training and awareness programs to educate employees and stakeholders about their roles and responsibilities in incident response. Ensure that personnel are familiar with the CIRP, know how to recognise and report security incidents, and understand their role in maintaining a secure work environment.

9. **Testing and Exercising**: Conduct regular testing and exercising of the CIRP through tabletop exercises, simulation drills, and red team/blue team scenarios. Evaluate the effectiveness of the plan, identify weaknesses, and refine response procedures based on lessons learned from exercises.

10. **Continuous Improvement and Adaptation**: Maintain flexibility and adaptability in the CIRP to respond to evolving threats, technologies, and regulatory requirements. Regularly review and update the plan based on changes in the threat landscape, organisational structure, and business processes.

4.1.1 What is Cybersecurity Incident Response Plan?

Tutorial Activity 1:

A cyber security incident response plan is a documented framework that outlines the actions and procedures to be followed when a cyber security incident occurs.

It provides a structured approach for effectively responding to and managing security incidents to minimise their impact on an organisation's information systems and data.

The incident response plan serves as a roadmap for the organisation, detailing the roles and responsibilities of the incident response team, communication protocols, escalation procedures, and the necessary technical and operational measures to be taken during each stage of the incident response process.

It helps ensure a coordinated and consistent response to incidents, enhances incident detection and containment, and reduces the time required to recover from an attack or breach.

4.1.2 Describe the circumstances under which a cybersecurity incident response plan is implemented and provide an example.

Tutorial Activity 2

A cyber security incident response plan is used when an organisation **experiences** a **cyber security incident**.

A cyber security incident refers to **any adverse event** or activity that poses a threat to the confidentiality, integrity, or availability of an organisation's information systems and data.

This can include **unauthorised access, data breaches, malware infections**, network intrusions, denial-of-service attacks, and other security breaches.

When a cyber security incident occurs, the incident response plan is **activated** to guide the organisation's response **efforts**.

It provides a **systematic approach** for identifying, containing, eradicating, and recovering from the incident.

The plan ensures that the **incident is addressed promptly and effectively**, minimising the potential damage, and enabling the organisation to resume normal operations as quickly as possible. The incident response plan plays a critical role in ensuring the resilience and continuity of business operations in the face of security incidents and emergencies. It helps organisations minimise damage, restore normal operations quickly, and improve overall security posture by learning from past incidents and strengthening preventive measures.

Key breakdown points to take away are:

1. **Prompt and Effective Addressing of Incidents**: The incident response plan aims to ensure that when security incidents occur, they are dealt with promptly and effectively. This means having predefined procedures and workflows in place to respond to different types of incidents, whether they involve cybersecurity breaches, system failures, data breaches, or other emergencies.

2. **Minimising Potential Damage**: One of the primary goals of the incident response plan is to minimise the potential damage caused by security incidents. This includes limiting the scope of the incident, preventing further compromise of systems or data, and mitigating the impact on the organisation's operations, reputation, and stakeholders.

3. **Resuming Normal Operations Quickly**: The incident response plan is designed to facilitate the swift recovery of affected systems and services, enabling the

organisation to resume normal operations as quickly as possible. This involves identifying the root cause of the incident, implementing corrective measures, restoring data and services, and ensuring that any vulnerabilities or weaknesses that contributed to the incident are addressed to prevent future occurrences.

4. **MTBF (Mean Time Between Failures) and MTTR (Mean Time to Repair)**: MTBF refers to the average time between failures of a system or component, while MTTR refers to the average time it takes to repair a failed system or component. These metrics are used to measure the reliability and maintainability of systems and help organisations assess their ability to respond to and recover from incidents effectively. By knowing the MTBF and MTTR, organisations can better plan and allocate resources for incident response and recovery efforts.

4.1.3 Describe the stages of a cybersecurity incident response lifecycle.

Tutorial Activity 3

Various lifecycle frameworks exist, e.g., NIST, SANS

The NIST (National Institute of Standards and Technology) framework provides a comprehensive approach to managing and responding to cybersecurity incidents.

The incident response lifecycle consists of **four** stages:
1. **Preparation:** The preparation stage involves activities that help organisations proactively prepare for potential cybersecurity incidents. Key tasks include:

    - **Developing an incident response plan (IRP):** Creating a documented plan that outlines the organisation's procedures, roles, and responsibilities during an incident.

    - **Establishing an incident response team (IRT):** Identifying and training a team of individuals with specific roles and responsibilities for incident response.

    - **Conducting risk assessments:** Assessing the organisation's assets, vulnerabilities, and potential threats to determine the level of risk.

    - **Implementing security controls:** Deploying preventive measures such as firewalls, intrusion detection systems, and access controls.

    - **Establishing communication channels:** Setting up communication channels for internal and external stakeholders during an incident.

2. **Detection and Analysis:** This stage focuses on identifying and understanding potential cybersecurity incidents. Activities include:

    - **Implementing monitoring systems:** Setting up tools and processes to monitor networks, systems, and applications for signs of malicious activities.

    - **Gathering and analysing data:** Collecting and analysing relevant data to identify indicators of compromise (IOCs) or abnormal activities.

    - **Verifying incidents:** Determining the nature and severity of identified incidents and validating their legitimacy.

    - **Classifying incidents:** Categorising incidents based on their impact, priority, and type for appropriate response prioritisation.

3. **Containment, Eradication, and Recovery:** Once an incident is detected and analysed, the organisation must take immediate action to contain and mitigate the impact. Key steps include:

    - **Containment:** Isolating affected systems, disconnecting from networks, and implementing access controls to prevent further spread.

    - **Eradication:** Identifying the root cause of the incident, removing malicious code or files, and patching vulnerabilities.

    - **Recovery:** Restoring affected systems to a known secure state and verifying their integrity before reconnecting to the network.

    - **Lessons learned:** Documenting all actions taken during containment, eradication, and recovery for future reference and improvement.

4. **Post-Incident Activity:** This stage focuses on reviewing the incident response process and improving the organisation's overall security posture. Key activities include:

    - **Post-incident analysis:** Conducting a thorough analysis of the incident, including its causes, impact, and effectiveness of the response.

    - **Reporting and communication:** Preparing incident reports for management, stakeholders, and regulatory bodies, as required.

    - **Updating incident response plan:** Incorporating lessons learned from the incident into the IRP to enhance future incident response capabilities.

    - **Training and awareness:** Conducting training sessions for employees to raise awareness of cybersecurity threats and incident response procedures.

4.2 Develop the capability to mitigate or eliminate potential cybersecurity vulnerabilities.

4.2.1 Why is it important to maintain an up-to-date cybersecurity incident log.

It is important to maintain an up-to-date cyber security incident log for several reasons:

- **Recordkeeping**: An incident log serves as a centralised repository of all security incidents and their related details. It captures information such as the date and time of the incident, the nature of the incident, the systems or assets affected, the actions taken, and the outcomes. This log becomes a valuable source of information for future reference, analysis, and reporting purposes.

- **Trend analysis:** By maintaining an incident log over time, organisations can identify patterns, trends, and common vulnerabilities or attack vectors. This analysis can help in understanding the organisation's security posture, identifying recurring issues, and implementing preventive measures to address them effectively.

- **Compliance and regulatory requirements:** Many industries and jurisdictions have specific requirements for incident reporting and recordkeeping. Maintaining an up-to-date incident log ensures that organisations can meet these compliance obligations and provide evidence of their incident response activities when necessary.

- **Incident response improvement:** An incident log facilitates continuous improvement of the incident response process. By reviewing past incidents, organisations can identify areas where the response could have been more effective, where additional training or resources may be required, or where changes to policies and procedures are needed. This analysis helps organisations refine their incident response capabilities and strengthen their overall security posture.

4.2.2 Outline the procedures to incorporate into a cybersecurity incident response plan.

- **Preparation:**
    - Define the incident response team roles and responsibilities.
    - Establish communication and escalation procedures.
    - Identify and prioritise critical assets and systems.
    - Implement preventive measures and security controls.

- **Detection and analysis:**
    - Establish monitoring systems and processes.
    - Train employees on incident detection and reporting.
    - Establish procedures for incident triage and assessment.
- **Containment, eradication, and recovery:**
    - Define procedures for containing and isolating affected systems.
    - Develop steps for removing threats and restoring systems.
    - Establish backup and recovery procedures.
- **Investigation and analysis:**
    - Define procedures for conducting a forensic analysis.
    - Preserve and collect evidence.
    - Identify the root cause and vulnerability exploited.
- **Reporting and communication:**
    - Establish procedures for reporting incidents to stakeholders.
    - Determine the appropriate authorities or regulatory bodies to notify.
    - Define the content and format of incident reports.
- **Lessons learned and improvement:**
    - Conduct a post-incident analysis to identify areas for improvement.
    - Document lessons learned and recommendations.
    - Update the incident response plan based on the findings.

4.2.3 What is the significance of having a cybersecurity incident response plan?

It is important to have a cyber security incident response plan for the following reasons:

- **Preparedness:** A well-defined incident response plan ensures that an organisation is prepared to handle security incidents effectively. It establishes clear guidelines, roles, and responsibilities, enabling a timely and coordinated response.
- **Minimise impact:** An incident response plan helps minimise the impact of security incidents by providing a structured and systematic approach to contain, mitigate,

and recover from them. This reduces the potential damage to systems, data, and the organisation's reputation.

- **Faster response time:** Having a plan in place enables organisations to respond promptly to security incidents. The predefined procedures and communication channels help streamline the response efforts, reducing the time required to detect, analyse, and resolve incidents.

- **Consistency and compliance:** An incident response plan ensures that incidents are handled consistently across the organisation. It helps organisations meet legal, regulatory, and industry-specific compliance requirements related to incident reporting, recordkeeping, and response procedures.

- **Continuous improvement:** By documenting and analysing past incidents, an incident response plan facilitates continuous improvement of the organisation's security posture. It allows organisations to learn from their experiences, identify areas for improvement, and implement measures to enhance their incident response capabilities.

4.2.4 Develop a cybersecurity incident response plan for an organisation.

Developing a comprehensive cyber security incident response plan requires a detailed understanding of an organisation's specific needs, its resources, and industry regulations.

Without knowing these, a general template for a cybersecurity incident response plan may be considered and customised based on an organisation's requirements.

Effectiveness of the Incident Response Plan

To ensure effectiveness of the incident response plan, it is important to involve key stakeholders, such as IT, legal, HR, and senior management in the development and review of the plan and to align it with organisational goals.

- **Introduction and scope:**
    - Purpose of the plan
    - Scope and applicability
    - Key stakeholders and their roles

- **Incident response team:**
    - Roles and responsibilities
    - Contact information.
    - Reporting structure

- **Incident response procedures:**
    - Incident identification and reporting
    - Initial assessment and triage
    - Escalation procedures

- **Incident response phases:**
    - Preparation
    - Detection and analysis
    - Containment, eradication, and recovery
    - Investigation and analysis
    - Reporting and communication
    - Lessons learned and improvement.

- **Communication and coordination:**
    - Internal communication channels and procedures
    - External communication protocols (e.g., public relations, legal, regulatory bodies)

- **Technical response measures:**
    - Incident handling and containment
    - System recovery and restoration
    - Evidence collection and preservation

- **Legal and regulatory considerations:**
    - Applicable laws and regulations
    - Reporting obligations
    - Compliance requirements

- **Training and awareness:**
    - Employee training on incident response procedures
    - Awareness campaigns and best practices

- **Plan maintenance and testing:**
    - Plan review and updates.
    - Testing and exercises
    - Performance metrics and evaluation

- **Appendices:**
    - Incident reporting templates
    - Contact lists.
    - References and resources

Case Study 1

A medium-sized family-owned manufacturing company relied heavily on online banking. Employees were required to log in using both a unique company ID and their personal credentials. Additionally, for any transactions exceeding £5,000, they had to answer two challenge questions.

One fateful day, the company owner received a notification about an unauthorised transfer of £20,000 from an unfamiliar source. Immediately, they contacted the bank and were stunned to discover that over the course of just one-week, cyber criminals had executed six transfers from the company's accounts, amassing a staggering £800,000. Subsequent investigation revealed that an employee had unwittingly opened an email they believed was from a trusted supplier of raw materials, only to find it harboured malware from an imposter source.

The attackers managed to infiltrate the company's computer systems, deploying a keylogger to pilfer vital banking credentials. Armed with this information, they gained entry to the company's online banking and financial services, wielding legitimate account numbers and passwords.

In the initial weeks following the breach, the bank managed to recover only £300,000 of the pilfered funds, resulting in a substantial loss of £500,000. The absence of a robust cyber security protocol hindered the company's ability to swiftly counter the fraudulent activity.

In response, the company took decisive action, closing their compromised bank account and initiating legal proceedings to recoup their losses.

Solution to Case Study 1

Introduction

This case study examines a cybersecurity breach that occurred at a medium-sized family-owned manufacturing company.

The company regularly used online banking for financial transactions but fell victim to a cyberattack, resulting in a significant financial loss.

The incident highlights the importance of having robust cybersecurity measures in place to protect against such threats.

Background

The construction company relied on online banking, where employees logged in using both a company and user-specific ID and password.

To enhance security, the system also required employees to answer two challenge questions for transactions exceeding £5,000.

The Cyber Attack

One day, the company owner received a notification about an unauthorised transfer of £20,000 initiated by an unknown source.

Further investigation revealed that over a one-week period, cyber criminals had executed six transfers totalling £800,000 from the company's bank accounts.

It was discovered that an employee had unknowingly opened an email that appeared to be from a materials supplier but contained malware from an imposter account.

Immediate Response

Upon discovering the breach, the company promptly contacted the bank to report the fraudulent transfers.

The bank was able to recover only £300,000 of the stolen funds in the first weeks, leaving the company with a significant financial loss of £500,000.

Unfortunately, the absence of a formal cybersecurity plan hampered the company's ability to respond effectively to the incident.

Mitigation Measures

To mitigate further damage, the construction company took immediate action by shutting down its bank account and pursuing legal recourse to recover the remaining losses.

However, the absence of a well-defined cybersecurity plan caused delays in the company's response, potentially exacerbating the impact of the breach.

Lessons Learned:

The case study highlights several key lessons for organisations to enhance their cybersecurity posture:

   a. **Employee Awareness:** Employees must be educated on cybersecurity best practices, including how to identify and avoid phishing emails, suspicious attachments, and malicious links.

   b. **Robust Cybersecurity Measures:** It is crucial to implement comprehensive cybersecurity measures, such as anti-malware software, firewalls, and regular software updates, to prevent and detect cyber threats.

   c. **Strong Password Policies:** Implementing strong password policies, including multi-factor authentication, can significantly reduce the risk of unauthorised access to sensitive systems.

   d. **Incident Response Plan:** Having a well-defined incident response plan in place can help organisations respond swiftly and effectively to cyberattacks, minimising the potential impact and financial losses.

   e. **Regular Training and Testing:** Conducting regular cybersecurity training sessions and simulated phishing exercises can help employees stay vigilant and reinforce safe online practices.

   f. **Collaboration with Financial Institutions:** Establishing a proactive relationship with the bank and other financial institutions can aid in swift response and recovery in the event of a cyber-attack.

Conclusion

This case study emphasizes the importance of cybersecurity ***preparedness*** for businesses of all sizes.

By implementing robust security measures, educating employees, and having a ***well-defined incident response plan***, organisations can better protect themselves against cyber threats and mitigate potential financial losses.

4.3 Be able to develop an incident post-mortem report.

4.3.1 What is an incident post-mortem?

Incident post-mortem refers to the process of conducting a thorough analysis and review of a security incident after it has been resolved.

It involves examining the incident, identifying its root causes, assessing the effectiveness of the incident response process, and making recommendations to prevent similar incidents in the future.

The goal of an incident post-mortem is to learn from the incident and improve the organisation's security posture.

4.3.2 The structure of an incident post-mortem.

The structure of an incident post-mortem report may vary depending on the organisation's preferences and requirements. Nonetheless, a typical structure includes the following sections:

- **Executive summary:** Provides a concise overview of the incident, its impact, and the key findings and recommendations.

- **Incident background:** Describes the incident in detail, including the date and time of occurrence, the systems or assets affected, the attack vectors or vulnerabilities exploited, and any initial actions taken.

- **Incident response assessment:** Evaluates the effectiveness of the incident response process, including the timeliness of response, the coordination among teams, and the adherence to procedures outlined in the incident response plan.

- **Root cause analysis:** Identifies the underlying causes and contributing factors that led to the incident. This section analyses any vulnerabilities, misconfigurations, human errors, or procedural gaps that were exploited by the attackers.

- **Impact assessment:** Assesses the impact of the incident on the organisation, such as financial losses, data breaches, operational disruptions, reputational damage, or regulatory non-compliance.

- **Findings and recommendations:** Presents the main findings from the incident analysis and provides actionable recommendations to prevent similar incidents in the future. Recommendations may include technical measures, policy changes, employee training, or process improvements.

- **Lessons learned:** Summarises the key lessons learned from the incident, highlighting areas for improvement in the incident response process, security controls, and overall security posture.

- **Appendices:** Includes any supporting documentation, such as incident logs, technical analysis reports, communication records, or evidence collected during the investigation.

4.3.3 The importance of integrity, rigour and discipline when carrying out an incident **post-mortem.**

When carrying out an incident post-mortem, the following factors are important:

- **Integrity:** Ensuring the integrity of the incident post-mortem process involves conducting an unbiased and transparent analysis. It is crucial to accurately represent the facts, findings, and recommendations without any undue influence or manipulation. This helps build trust in the process and ensures that the insights gained are reliable and credible.

- **Rigour:** A rigorous approach involves conducting a comprehensive analysis and investigation. It includes collecting and examining all available evidence, conducting a thorough root cause analysis, and considering multiple perspectives. Rigour helps uncover underlying issues and provides a solid foundation for developing effective recommendations.

- **Discipline:** Maintaining discipline throughout the post-mortem process ensures consistency and adherence to established procedures. It involves following a structured approach, documenting all steps, and involving the appropriate stakeholders. Discipline helps prevent overlooking important details and ensures that the post-mortem process is repeatable and consistent over time.

4.3.4 Create a post-mortem report of an incident.

Reference: Case Study 1

Post-Mortem Report: Cybersecurity Breach at a Medium-sized Family-Owned Manufacturing Company

1. Incident Overview

Recently, a cybersecurity breach occurred at a medium-sized family-owned manufacturing company, resulting in unauthorised transfers totalling £800,000 from the company's bank accounts.

The incident was caused by an employee inadvertently opening a malicious email, leading to the installation of malware on the company's computers.

The attackers used keylogging techniques to capture banking credentials and gain access to online banking and financial services.

The company's lack of a cybersecurity plan delayed their response to the fraud, resulting in a loss of £500,000.

2. Timeline of Events

Incident Overview: Recently, a cybersecurity breach occurred at a medium-sized family-owned manufacturing company, resulting in unauthorised transfers totalling £800,000 from the company's bank accounts. The incident was caused by an employee inadvertently opening a malicious email, leading to the installation of malware on the company's computers.

The attackers used keylogging techniques to capture banking credentials and gain access to online banking and financial services. The company's lack of a cybersecurity plan delayed their response to the fraud, resulting in a loss of £500,000.

3. Root Causes

Lack of Employee Awareness: The employee's lack of awareness regarding phishing emails and their inability to identify the malicious email resulted in the initial breach.

Insufficient Cybersecurity Measures: The absence of robust cybersecurity measures, such as anti-malware software and firewalls, allowed the malware to infiltrate the company's systems undetected.

Weak Password Security: Inadequate password policies and the absence of multi-factor authentication facilitated the attackers' unauthorised access to the company's online banking accounts.

Absence of a Cybersecurity Plan: The lack of a formal cybersecurity plan and incident response procedures delayed the company's response to the incident and impeded their ability to mitigate the damage.

4. Impact Analysis

Financial Loss: The company suffered a loss of £500,000 because of the fraudulent transfers, with only £300,000 recovered by the bank.

Reputational Damage: The incident may have negatively impacted on the company's reputation, as clients and business partners could lose trust in its ability to secure sensitive information.

Legal Consequences: Pursuing legal action to recover the remaining losses incurred, additional costs and could have potential long-term legal implications.

5. Lessons Learned

Employee Training and Awareness: Employees must receive regular training on identifying and avoiding phishing emails, suspicious attachments, and malicious links to prevent similar incidents.

Robust Cybersecurity Measures: Implementing strong cybersecurity measures, including anti-malware software, firewalls, and regular software updates, is crucial to detect and prevent cyber threats.

Password Security: Enforce strong password policies and implement multi-factor authentication to enhance the security of online accounts.

Incident Response Planning: Develop and maintain a comprehensive cybersecurity plan and incident response procedures to ensure a timely and effective response to future incidents.

Collaboration with Financial Institutions: Establish a proactive relationship with the bank and other financial institutions to facilitate a swift response and recovery in the event of a cyberattack.

6. Recommendations

Implement Security Awareness Training: Conduct regular training sessions to educate employees about cybersecurity best practices and raise awareness of potential threats.

Strengthen Cybersecurity Infrastructure: Deploy robust security measures such as firewalls, anti-malware software, and intrusion detection systems to protect against future attacks.

Enhance Password Policies: Enforce strong password policies that include regular password updates and multi-factor authentication for all critical systems and accounts.

Develop an Incident Response Plan: Create a comprehensive incident response plan that outlines roles, responsibilities, and actions to be taken in the event of a cybersecurity incident.

Regular Security Audits: Conduct periodic security audits and vulnerability assessments to identify and address any weaknesses in the company's IT infrastructure.

Engage Legal Counsel: Seek legal advice to understand the company's options and potential legal actions to recover losses and protect against future incidents.

Conclusion

The cybersecurity breach at the medium-sized family-owned manufacturing company serves as a reminder of the importance of implementing strong cybersecurity measures and maintaining an incident response plan.

By improving employee awareness, implementing robust security controls, and having a proactive cybersecurity approach, organisations can reduce the risk of cyberattacks, mitigate potential financial losses, and safeguard their reputation and client trust.

Case Study 2

Tutorial Activity: XYZ Ltd., a prominent enterprise, recently fell victim to a significant Ransomware attack that encrypted critical folders and files, constituting a severe breach of their cybersecurity. The organisation found itself compelled to make a ransom payment to regain access to their essential documents.

In your capacity as a cybersecurity expert, you've been entrusted with the responsibility of formulating a retrospective report on this incident.

Post-Mortem Report - an example of a post-mortem report for Case Study 2 incident.

- Executive Summary:
    - Overview of the incident, impact, and key findings.
    - Summary of recommendations for improvement.

- Incident Background:
    - Date, time, and duration of the incident.
    - Systems or assets affected.
    - Initial response actions taken.

- Incident Response Assessment:
    - Evaluation of the incident response process.
    - Assessment of response timeliness, coordination, and effectiveness.

- Identification of strengths and areas for improvement.
- Root Cause Analysis:
    - Identification of the root causes and contributing factors.
    - Analysis of vulnerabilities, misconfigurations, or procedural gaps exploited.
    - Description of the attack vectors or techniques used.
- Impact Assessment:
    - Evaluation of the impact on the organisation.
    - Financial, operational, reputational, or regulatory implications.
    - Quantification of losses or damages incurred.
- Findings and Recommendations:
    - Summary of main findings from the incident analysis.
    - Actionable recommendations to prevent similar incidents.
    - Recommendations for technical controls, policy changes, training, or process improvements
- Lessons Learned:
    - Key lessons learned from the incident.
    - Identification of areas for improvement in incident response and security posture.
    - Strategies to enhance resilience and response capabilities.
- Appendices:
    - Incident logs, technical analysis reports, or other supporting documentation.
    - Communication records, evidence collected, or any relevant artifacts.

4.3.5 Reflect upon the post-mortem report and make recommendations based on the findings.

Reflecting upon the post-mortem report, it is important to consider the findings and recommendations to drive improvements in the organisation's security posture. Based on the report's findings, the following recommendations could be sufficient:

- **Strengthen vulnerability management:** Implement a regular vulnerability scanning and patch management process to address the identified vulnerabilities that were exploited in the incident.

- **Enhance employee training and awareness:** Conduct regular security awareness training sessions for employees to educate them about common attack vectors, social engineering techniques, and best practices for safeguarding sensitive information.

- **Improve incident response coordination:** Review and update the incident response plan to enhance coordination among different teams, ensure clear communication channels, and establish effective escalation procedures.

- **Implement network segmentation and access controls:** Separate critical systems and sensitive data from the rest of the network through network segmentation and enforce strict access controls to limit unauthorised access.

- **Strengthen monitoring and detection capabilities:** Enhance intrusion detection systems, log management, and security information and event management (SIEM) solutions to improve the detection and response to future incidents.

- **Conduct regular security assessments:** Perform periodic security assessments, including penetration testing and red team exercises, to proactively identify and address potential vulnerabilities and weaknesses in the organisation's defences.

- **Establish an incident response testing program:** Regularly test the incident response plan through tabletop exercises and simulated incident scenarios to ensure preparedness and identify areas for improvement.

- **Review incident communication protocols:** Assess the effectiveness of communication during the incident and update communication protocols to ensure timely and accurate dissemination of information to stakeholders.

- **Enhance incident logging and documentation:** Improve incident logging practices to capture critical details, timestamps, and actions taken during the incident response process for future reference and analysis.

- **Establish a lesson learned repository:** Create a central repository to document and share lessons learned from incidents, ensuring that the organisation can benefit from past experiences and prevent similar incidents in the future.

Conclusion

That been said, the post-mortem report should be addressed to the specific findings and needs of your organisation and involve relevant stakeholders in the implementation of the recommendations. Use SMART, SWOT techniques.

4.4 Integrating SMART, SWOT Techniques.

Incorporating SMART (Specific, Measurable, Achievable, Relevant, Time-bound) and SWOT (Strengths, Weaknesses, Opportunities, Threats) techniques into the development and analysis of a Cybersecurity Incident Response Plan (CIRP). By integrating SMART objectives and SWOT analysis into the development and analysis of the Cybersecurity Incident Response Plan, organisations can enhance their incident response capabilities, mitigate risks, and improve overall cybersecurity resilience.

SMART Technique

1. **Specific:**
    - Clearly define the objectives and goals of the CIRP, such as:
        1. Rapid detection and containment of security incidents.
        2. Minimisation of downtime and service disruptions.
        3. Preservation of data integrity and confidentiality.

2. **Measurable:**
    - Define key performance indicators (KPIs) to measure the effectiveness of the CIRP, such as:
        1. Mean time to detect (MTTD) security incidents.
        2. Mean time to respond (MTTR) to security incidents.
        3. Percentage reduction in incident recurrence.

3. **Achievable:**
    - Ensure that the goals and objectives set for the CIRP are realistic and attainable given the organisation's resources, capabilities, and infrastructure.
    - Align the CIRP with the organisation's risk tolerance and compliance requirements.

4. **Relevant:**
    - Ensure that the CIRP is aligned with the organisation's overall cybersecurity strategy, business objectives, and industry best practices.
    - Address specific threats and vulnerabilities relevant to the organisation's IT environment and industry sector.

5. **Time-bound**:
    - Establish clear timelines and deadlines for key activities and milestones within the CIRP, such as:
        1. Quarterly tabletop exercises to test the effectiveness of the CIRP.
        2. Annual review and update of the CIRP based on lessons learned and emerging threats.

SWOT Analysis
1. **Strengths**:
    1. Established incident response team with defined roles and responsibilities.
    2. Robust communication protocols for internal and external stakeholders.
    3. Regular training and awareness programs to educate employees about security best practices.
2. **Weaknesses**:
    1. Lack of dedicated resources and funding for incident response activities.
    2. Limited integration and coordination between IT, security, and other business units.
    3. Inadequate testing and validation of the CIRP's effectiveness in real-world scenarios.
3. **Opportunities**:
    1. Adoption of emerging technologies such as AI and machine learning for automated incident detection and response.
    2. Collaboration with industry peers and information-sharing networks to gain insights into emerging threats and vulnerabilities.
    3. Integration of threat intelligence feeds and security analytics platforms to enhance incident detection capabilities.
4. **Threats**:
    1. Increasing sophistication of cyber threats, including ransomware, phishing attacks, and insider threats.
    2. Regulatory compliance requirements and potential fines for data breaches and security incidents.

3. Shortage of skilled cybersecurity professionals and talent retention challenges.

Integration:
- Leverage strengths to capitalise on opportunities and address weaknesses and threats.
- Develop strategies and action plans to mitigate identified weaknesses and threats while maximising strengths and opportunities.
- Regularly review and update the CIRP based on insights from the SWOT analysis and SMART objectives to ensure its effectiveness and adaptability to changing cyber threats and organisational needs.

Chapter 5: Cybersecurity: Legislation, Trends, and Ethical Considerations

Learning Outcome:
- **5.1 Understand legislation relating to cybersecurity.**
    - Describe how legislation impacts on cybersecurity.
    - Explain trends in international law for cyberspace.
- **5.2 Understand information security standards.**
    - Identify ISO standards related to cybersecurity.
    - Explain how ISO standards are used to support cyber security.
- **5.3 Understand ethical conduct within cybersecurity.**
    - Describe ethical conduct within cybersecurity.
    - Identify unethical conduct within cybersecurity.

5. About this chapter

In Chapter 5, "Legislation, Trends, and Ethics in Cybersecurity," readers embark on a journey through the intricate interplay of legal frameworks, international trends, and ethical considerations that define the ever-evolving landscape of cybersecurity.

The chapter commences by unravelling the impact of legislation on cybersecurity practices. It underscores the pivotal role of laws in shaping rules, responsibilities, and rights within jurisdictions. Delving into critical areas such as data protection, cybercrime prevention, security standards, and international cooperation, the chapter examines how legislation influences and regulates the cybersecurity landscape. Real-world examples, including the Computer Misuse Act and GDPR, illustrate the profound impact of legal frameworks on safeguarding sensitive information and deterring cyber threats.

A spotlight is then cast on emerging trends in international law for cyberspace. Regional initiatives, exemplified by the European Union's cohesive approach to harmonising data protection and cybersecurity regulations, and the ASEAN Cybersecurity Cooperation Strategy, demonstrate the collaborative efforts to address the complex challenges of cyberspace. The chapter emphasizes the growing importance of attribution and accountability, acknowledging the challenges posed by the transnational nature of cyber threats.

Shifting gears, the narrative unfolds to introduce the pivotal role of ISO standards in fortifying cybersecurity measures. Readers gain insights into key ISO standards, including

ISO/IEC 27001 and ISO/IEC 27032, and how these globally recognised benchmarks offer a structured approach to risk management and best practices. The chapter illuminates how adherence to ISO standards not only enhances cybersecurity posture but also fosters international collaboration and trade.

Finally, the chapter delves into the ethical considerations within the realm of cybersecurity. It outlines a spectrum of ethical principles guiding professionals and organisations towards responsible and morally upright conduct. From maintaining confidentiality and promoting information security to continuous learning and ethical decision-making, the chapter articulates the core tenets that underpin ethical conduct. In parallel, it identifies unethical behaviours, such as sabotage and unauthorised access, that compromise the integrity, privacy, and security of individuals and organisations.

In essence, Chapter 5 offers readers a multifaceted exploration of the legal, international, and ethical dimensions of cybersecurity. By navigating through the intricacies of legislation, trends, and ethical conduct, readers gain a comprehensive understanding of the frameworks that define and safeguard the digital realm.

5.1 Understand legislation relating to cyber security.

Legislation is a cornerstone in shaping and regulating cybersecurity practices. It establishes the rules, rights, and responsibilities within a particular jurisdiction. In the realm of cybersecurity, legislation impacts various critical areas.

5.1.1 Legislation as it impacts on cybersecurity.

1. **Data Protection and Privacy:** Legislation such as the General Data Protection Regulation (GDPR) in the UK and European Union, and the California Consumer Privacy Act (CCPA) in the United States, impose legal obligations on organisations. They are required to protect personal data and ensure the privacy rights of individuals. This includes implementing appropriate security measures, conducting risk assessments, and notifying individuals in the event of a data breach.

2. **Cybercrime Prevention:** Laws such as the Computer Fraud and Abuse Act (CFAA) in the United States and the Council of Europe Convention on Cybercrime (Budapest Convention) criminalise various cyber offenses. This includes activities like hacking, unauthorised access, identity theft, and distributed denial-of-service (DDoS) attacks. These laws empower law enforcement agencies to investigate and prosecute cybercriminals, thereby deterring cyber-attacks.

3. **Security Standards and Compliance:** Legislation may establish security standards and frameworks that organisations must adhere to. For example, the Payment Card Industry Data Security Standard (PCI DSS) mandates security requirements for businesses that process credit card transactions. Non-compliance with such standards can result in penalties, fines, and legal consequences.

4. **National Security and Critical Infrastructure Protection:** Governments often enact legislation to protect national security interests and critical infrastructure from cyber threats. These laws may include provisions for the establishment of cybersecurity agencies, intelligence sharing, and regulation of sectors like telecommunications, energy, and finance to ensure the resilience of essential services.

5. **International Cooperation:** Legislation can facilitate international cooperation in cybersecurity. Countries may pass laws to enhance information sharing, promote mutual assistance in investigating cybercrimes, and establish mechanisms for cross-border cooperation in tackling cyber threats. This can take the form of bilateral agreements, multilateral treaties, and participation in international organisations like the United Nations and the International Telecommunication Union.

Impact of Legislation on Cybersecurity

Legislation plays a significant role in shaping and influencing cybersecurity practices across various sectors and jurisdictions. The impact of legislation on cybersecurity can be profound, affecting organisations, individuals, and society in several ways:

1. **Regulatory Compliance**: Legislation often mandates specific cybersecurity requirements that organisations must adhere to, such as data protection laws, industry regulations, and government mandates. For example, laws like the General Data Protection Regulation (GDPR) in the United Kingdom/European Union and the Health Insurance Portability and Accountability Act (HIPAA) in the United States impose strict requirements for the protection of personal and sensitive data. Compliance with these regulations not only helps mitigate legal risks but also fosters trust among customers and stakeholders.

2. **Increased Accountability**: Cybersecurity legislation holds organisations accountable for safeguarding sensitive information and maintaining the integrity, confidentiality, and availability of data assets. This accountability extends to executives, board members, and other stakeholders who may face legal consequences for breaches resulting from negligence or non-compliance with regulatory requirements. As a result, organisations are incentivised to invest in

robust cybersecurity measures and governance frameworks to mitigate risks and ensure regulatory compliance.

3. **Enhanced Cybersecurity Standards**: Legislation often establishes minimum cybersecurity standards and best practices that organisations must follow to protect against evolving cyber threats. These standards may cover areas such as network security, data encryption, incident response planning, and risk management. By setting clear expectations and guidelines, legislation helps raise the overall level of cybersecurity maturity across industries and promotes a culture of security awareness and accountability.

4. **Cross-Border Cooperation**: In an increasingly interconnected world, cyber threats transcend national borders, making international collaboration and information sharing essential for effective cybersecurity. Legislation can facilitate cross-border cooperation by establishing frameworks for mutual assistance, data sharing, and law enforcement cooperation in combating cybercrime and addressing cybersecurity incidents that span multiple jurisdictions.

5. **Resource Allocation and Funding**: Legislation may allocate resources and funding for cybersecurity initiatives, research, and capacity-building efforts at the national and international levels. Government agencies, regulatory bodies, and law enforcement agencies may receive funding to develop cybersecurity strategies, establish cybersecurity centres of excellence, and support cybersecurity education and training programs. Additionally, legislation may provide incentives, grants, or tax breaks to encourage private sector investment in cybersecurity technologies and solutions.

6. **Legal and Regulatory Challenges**: Despite the benefits of cybersecurity legislation, there are also challenges and complexities associated with compliance, enforcement, and interpretation of laws and regulations. Compliance requirements may vary across jurisdictions, leading to compliance burdens and regulatory fragmentation for multinational organisations operating in multiple countries. Additionally, rapid advancements in technology and evolving cyber threats may outpace the pace of legislative and regulatory reforms, requiring continuous updates and adaptations to address emerging challenges effectively.

Quiz: Impact of legislation on cybersecurity:

1. **What role does legislation play in cybersecurity?**
    a) Setting international cybersecurity standards
    b) Influencing cybersecurity practices through regulatory requirements
    c) Providing cybersecurity training for professionals
    d) Developing new cybersecurity technologies.

2. **Which of the following is NOT a potential impact of legislation on cybersecurity?**
    a) Regulatory compliance requirements
    b) Decreased accountability for organizations
    c) Enhanced cybersecurity standards
    d) Increased cross-border cooperation

3. **Which legislation imposes strict requirements for the protection of personal and sensitive data in the European Union?**
    a) HIPAA
    b) GDPR
    c) SOX
    d) FISMA

4. **What does compliance with cybersecurity legislation help to foster among customers and stakeholders?**
    a) Increased risk tolerance
    b) Trust
    c) Decreased accountability
    d) Legal challenges

5. **What is one way that legislation contribute to enhanced cybersecurity standards?** a) By reducing accountability for organizations
    b) By establishing minimum cybersecurity requirements
    c) By limiting cross-border cooperation
    d) By decreasing resources and funding for cybersecurity initiatives.

6. **Which of the following is a potential challenge associated with cybersecurity legislation?**
    a) Increased cross-border cooperation
    b) Fragmentation of regulatory requirements for multinational organizations

c) Decreased compliance burdens
d) Slow pace of legislative reforms

7. **What aspect of cybersecurity legislation may help address international cyber threats?**
   a) Compliance with local regulations
   b) Resource allocation and funding
   c) Legal and regulatory challenges
   d) Enforcement of cybersecurity standards

8. **What incentive might cybersecurity legislation provide to encourage private sector investment in cybersecurity technologies?**
   a) Tax breaks
   b) Increased penalties for non-compliance
   c) Reduced accountability
   d) Compliance burdens

9. **What is a potential outcome of effective cybersecurity legislation?**
   a) Decreased trust in digital ecosystems
   b) Regulatory fragmentation
   c) Enhanced cybersecurity resilience
   d) Decreased accountability for executives

10. **What is a key aspect of legislation that influences cybersecurity practices?**
    a) Ignoring international standards
    b) Establishing clear guidelines and requirements
    c) Avoiding resource allocation
    d) Decreasing cross-border cooperation

Typical examples of legislation that significantly impact cybersecurity.

1. Computer Misuse Act 1990

- *Purpose*: The Computer Misuse Act in the UK criminalises unauthorised access to computer systems, as well as activities like hacking, malware distribution, and denial-of-service attacks.

- *Impact on Cybersecurity*: It provides a legal framework to prosecute individuals involved in computer-related offenses. This law helps protect computer networks and sensitive information from unauthorised access and malicious activities.

2. Official Secrets Act 1989

- *Purpose*: The Official Secrets Act in the UK is designed to protect national security. It governs the handling of sensitive government information and imposes legal consequences for unauthorised disclosure or misuse of official secrets.

- *Impact on Cybersecurity*: It plays a vital role in safeguarding classified information, ensuring that sensitive government data is not compromised or disclosed to unauthorised parties.

3. Communications Act 2003

- *Purpose*: The Communications Act in the UK provides a regulatory framework for the communication industry. It covers various aspects of communication, including telecommunications, broadcasting, and the internet.

- *Impact on Cybersecurity*: The Act includes provisions related to the interception of communications, network security, and ensuring the proper functioning and safety of communication services. It helps regulate and secure the digital communication landscape.

4. Data Protection Act 2018/UK General Data Protection Regulation (UK GDPR)

- *Purpose*: These laws in the UK govern the collection, storage, processing, and transfer of personal data. They outline individuals' rights regarding their personal information and impose obligations on organisations to handle data securely, obtain consent, and notify individuals about data breaches.

- *Impact on Cybersecurity*: They establish robust requirements for data protection and privacy, mandating organisations to implement appropriate security measures. Non-compliance can lead to significant fines, incentivising organisations to invest in cybersecurity.

5. Police and Criminal Evidence Act 1984 (PACE)

- *Purpose*: PACE in the UK sets out the powers and procedures for police officers when dealing with criminal offenses. It regulates the arrest, detention, questioning, and evidence gathering processes to ensure fair treatment of suspects and the protection of their rights during investigations.

- *Impact on Cybersecurity*: PACE ensures that law enforcement agencies follow proper procedures in cybercrime investigations, upholding legal and ethical standards in the process.

6. Directive on security of network and information systems (2016/1148) (known as the NIS Directive)

- *Purpose*: This European Union legislation aims at enhancing the security of network and information systems within member states. It requires operators of essential services and digital service providers to implement appropriate security measures and report significant cyber incidents to national authorities.

- *Impact on Cybersecurity*: The NIS Directive strengthens cybersecurity measures, particularly for critical infrastructure. It ensures the resilience of essential services and promotes a coordinated response to cyber incidents.

These legislations collectively create a comprehensive legal framework for cybersecurity in the UK and the European Union. They address various aspects, including data protection, cybercrime prevention, communication security, and critical infrastructure protection. Compliance with these laws is crucial for organisations and individuals to maintain legal and ethical standards in the realm of cybersecurity.

5.1.2 Trends in international law for cyberspace.

Regional Initiatives

Regional organisations and initiatives play a critical role in addressing the complex and interconnected nature of cyberspace challenges. These efforts aim to foster cooperation among neighbouring countries, share best practices, and create a unified front against cyber threats. Two prominent examples of such regional initiatives are the European Union's endeavours to harmonise data protection and cybersecurity regulations, and the ASEAN Cybersecurity Cooperation Strategy:

European Union (EU) Initiatives

The European Union has taken significant strides towards harmonising data protection and cybersecurity regulations across its member states. This concerted effort is driven by several key objectives:

- **Unified Approach:** The EU aims to establish a unified approach to cybersecurity within its member states. By aligning regulations and standards, the EU seeks to create a cohesive and robust cybersecurity framework that spans across national borders.

- **Enhanced Resilience:** The harmonisation of data protection and cybersecurity regulations enhances the overall resilience of the EU region to cyber threats. This unified front allows for more effective detection, prevention, and response to cyber incidents, as well as a coordinated approach to incident management.

- **Streamlined Compliance:** Standardised regulations simplify compliance efforts for organisations operating within the EU. This reduces the administrative burden and ensures that companies can adhere to a consistent set of cybersecurity requirements across multiple jurisdictions.

- **Information Sharing and Cooperation:** The harmonisation efforts facilitate increased information sharing and cooperation among EU member states. This collective approach allows for timely threat intelligence sharing and coordinated responses to cyber incidents, ultimately strengthening the region's cybersecurity posture.

Association of Southeast Asian Nations (ASEAN) Cybersecurity Cooperation Strategy

ASEAN, a regional intergovernmental organisation comprising ten Southeast Asian countries, has recognised the importance of collective action in the realm of cybersecurity. The ASEAN Cybersecurity Cooperation Strategy is a significant initiative that underscores the following key points:

- **Supporting Regional Collaboration:** The ASEAN Cybersecurity Cooperation Strategy aims to enhance regional collaboration in addressing cybersecurity challenges. It provides a framework for member states to work together in areas such as threat intelligence sharing, incident response, and capacity building.

- **Capacity Building and Knowledge Sharing:** The strategy places a strong emphasis on capacity building, aiming to strengthen the cybersecurity capabilities of member states. This includes training programs, workshops, and knowledge-sharing initiatives to improve the technical expertise and awareness of cyber threats within the region.

- **Policy Coordination:** The strategy facilitates policy coordination among ASEAN member states, ensuring a unified and consistent approach to cybersecurity. This helps in aligning regulatory frameworks and standards across the region.

- **Promoting a Secure Digital Environment:** By focusing on cooperation, capacity building, and policy coordination, ASEAN's strategy ultimately aims to create a secure digital environment for its member states. This environment is conducive to economic growth, innovation, and the protection of critical infrastructure.

Attribution and Accountability

The issue of attribution in cyberspace refers to the ability to accurately identify the source or actor behind a cyber-attack. This is a critical aspect of international law discussions related to cybersecurity. Proper attribution is essential for several reasons:

1. **Accountability:** Attributing cyber-attacks to specific actors or states is crucial for holding them accountable for their actions. This accountability is essential in establishing consequences for malicious behaviour in cyberspace, deterring future attacks, and upholding international norms.

2. **Legal Response:** Accurate attribution is necessary for legal responses to cyber incidents. It enables affected parties or states to take appropriate legal actions against the responsible actors, whether through domestic or international legal channels.

3. **Deterrence:** Knowing that they can be held accountable, potential attackers may be less inclined to engage in cyber-attacks. This serves as a deterrent, potentially reducing the frequency and severity of cyber incidents.

4. **Norms and Rules:** Attribution helps reinforce international norms and rules regarding state behaviour in cyberspace. It clarifies what constitutes unacceptable behaviour and establishes a basis for collective action against cyber threats.

However, there are significant challenges associated with technical attribution:

1. **Transnational Nature of Cyber-Attacks:** Cyberspace is inherently transnational. Attackers can operate from different jurisdictions, use anonymising technologies, and deploy tactics to obfuscate their origins. This makes it difficult to definitively trace cyber-attacks back to a specific source.

2. **False Flags and Deception:** Sophisticated threat actors may employ techniques like false flags or deception to mislead investigators and falsely attribute an attack to a different entity or state.

3. **Attribution Lag:** The process of attribution can be time-consuming, and in some cases, it may take a significant amount of time to conclusively attribute an attack. This lag can hinder timely responses to cyber incidents.

4. **Technical Limitations:** Technical tools and methodologies for attribution may have limitations, and there may not always be clear-cut evidence to definitively identify the perpetrator.

Trends in international law for cyberspace are adapting to the rapidly evolving digital landscape. The issue of attribution and accountability is gaining prominence, underscoring the importance of accurately identifying and holding responsible those behind cyber-attacks. While attribution is crucial for legal response, deterrence, and upholding international norms, the technical challenges and transnational nature of cyberspace present significant obstacles to achieving clear and unequivocal attribution in all cases. These trends highlight the dynamic and complex nature of international law in the context of cyberspace, emphasizing the need for ongoing efforts to address these challenges.

5.2 Introduction to ISO Standards and Their Role in Cybersecurity

The International Organisation for Standardisation (ISO) is an autonomous, non-governmental entity responsible for developing and publishing international standards across various industries and sectors. These standards are designed to ensure consistency, quality, and best practices in products, services, and processes worldwide. Comprising national standards organisations from diverse countries, ISO was established in 1947 and is dedicated to formulating and disseminating international standards that span numerous fields and/or domains.

ISO's central objective is to promote standardisation and ensure uniformity in products, services, and processes across international borders. The organisation's standards offer precise specifications and guidelines for a wide array of areas, including best practices, quality and environmental management systems, and information security management.

These standards are crafted through a collaborative process that involves technical committees, subject matter experts, industry representatives, and stakeholders from member nations. While ISO standards are voluntary and lack legal enforcement, they frequently serve as pivotal references for governments, organisations, and industries when establishing regulations and requirements.

The work of ISO significantly contributes to bolstering effectiveness, safety, compatibility, and sustainability in various domains. This, in turn, fosters international collaboration and expedites global trade by establishing common frameworks and criteria.

5.2.1 Key ISO Standards Related to Cybersecurity

1. **ISO/IEC 27001: Information Security Management System (ISMS)**
    1. *Purpose*: Provides guidelines for establishing, implementing, maintaining, and continually improving an ISMS, which includes processes for managing information security risks.
    2. *Impact on Cybersecurity*: Helps organisations identify and manage security risks, implement controls, and ensure the confidentiality, integrity, and availability of information assets.

2. **ISO/IEC 27002: Information Security Controls**
    1. *Purpose*: Offers a comprehensive set of guidelines and best practices for information security controls, providing a catalogue of controls that organisations can select based on their specific needs and risk profiles.
    2. *Impact on Cybersecurity*: Helps organisations implement effective information security controls to safeguard their information assets.

3. **ISO/IEC 27005: Risk Management in Information Security**
    1. *Purpose*: Provides a framework for identifying, assessing, and treating information security risks within an organisation, promoting a systematic approach to managing security risks.
    2. *Impact on Cybersecurity*: Helps organisations proactively manage security risks to protect their information assets.

4. **ISO/IEC 27017: Cloud Security**
    1. *Purpose*: Focuses on cloud security, offering guidelines for information security controls specific to cloud service providers and their customers.
    2. *Impact on Cybersecurity*: Ensures the secure and effective use of cloud services by addressing the unique challenges associated with cloud computing.

5. **ISO/IEC 27032: Cybersecurity Guidance**
    1. *Purpose*: Provides guidance on cybersecurity concepts, principles, and processes, including risk management and incident management.

2. *Impact on Cybersecurity*: Helps organisations establish effective cybersecurity frameworks, policies, and practices.

6. **ISO/IEC 22301: Business Continuity Management**

    1. *Purpose*: Focuses on business continuity management, outlining requirements for establishing and maintaining a system to protect against and recover from disruptive incidents, including cybersecurity incidents.

    2. *Impact on Cybersecurity*: Helps organisations prepare for and respond to cybersecurity incidents, ensuring business continuity.

5.2.2 How ISO Standards Support Cybersecurity

ISO standards play a crucial role in bolstering cybersecurity measures within organisations. They serve as a comprehensive framework comprising of meticulously crafted best practices, controls, and guidelines, all aimed at fortifying an organisation's overall cybersecurity posture.

One of the pivotal aspects emphasized by ISO standards is the adoption of robust risk management principles. This empowers organisations to proficiently identify, assess, and subsequently mitigate potential cybersecurity risks. By doing so, they are better equipped to safeguard their digital assets and sensitive information.

Furthermore, adherence to ISO standards signifies an organisation's unwavering commitment to cybersecurity. This dedication can lead to the attainment of certification, which in turn augments the organisation's credibility in the realm of cybersecurity. It acts as a testament to their proactive efforts in securing their digital landscape.

ISO standards also instigate a culture of perpetual improvement in cybersecurity practices. This encourages organisations to remain agile in the face of evolving threats and technological advancements. By staying adaptable, organisations are better positioned to stay ahead of potential cyber threats and proactively safeguard their digital assets.

Moreover, these standards offer a globally recognised and harmonised approach to cybersecurity. This fosters interoperability, promotes seamless information sharing, and encourages collaboration across various sectors and international boundaries. It creates a cohesive environment where organisations can work together to bolster cybersecurity measures on a global scale.

Organisations that wholeheartedly adopt and adhere to ISO standards, stand to significantly enhance their cybersecurity practices. This not only fortifies their own digital defences but also contributes to the creation of a safer and more secure digital environment for all stakeholders involved.

5.3 Understanding Ethical Conduct within Cybersecurity

Ethical conducts are collective principles that form the bedrock of moral behaviours within the field of cybersecurity, they guide professionals towards responsible and morally sound practices in their work.

5.3.1 Describe Ethical Conduct within Cybersecurity

Ethical conduct in the field of cybersecurity encompasses a broad spectrum of responsible and morally upright behaviours exhibited by both individuals and organisations. It is characterised by a set of guiding principles and standards that steer professionals towards acting in an ethical and responsible manner. While the following elements are not an exhaustive list, they are paramount to ethical conduct within cybersecurity:

1. **Maintaining Confidentiality:** Cybersecurity professionals are entrusted with the duty to honour the confidentiality of sensitive information. They must handle data with utmost care, ensuring that it is only disclosed on a need-to-know basis. Additionally, they are responsible for implementing measures to protect this information from unauthorised access or disclosure, establishing a foundation of trust and security.

2. **Adherence to Applicable Laws and Regulations:** Ethical conduct dictates strict adherence to all relevant laws, regulations, and standards pertaining to cybersecurity. This encompasses compliance with data protection laws, privacy regulations, intellectual property rights, and any other legal obligations governing the handling of information and cybersecurity practices.

3. **Promoting Information Security:** Ethical cybersecurity professionals bear the responsibility of championing information security within their respective organisations or for their clients. This involves the diligent implementation of appropriate security measures, conducting thorough risk assessments, and ensuring the integrity, availability, and confidentiality of information.

4. **Refraining from Conflicts of Interest:** Professionals must exercise vigilance in avoiding conflicts of interest that may compromise their objectivity, independence, or integrity. They are obliged to prioritise the best interests of their clients or organisations and, if necessary, disclose any potential conflicts to maintain transparency and preserve trust.

5. **Honesty and Integrity:** Ethical conduct necessitates that cybersecurity professionals conduct themselves with honesty and integrity in every facet of their work. This encompasses providing accurate information, being transparent about their actions and decisions, and upholding high ethical standards, thereby fostering an environment of trust and credibility.

6. **Informed Consent and Privacy:** Professionals must obtain informed consent from individuals when collecting and processing their data, ensuring that privacy rights are respected. They should clearly communicate the purpose, scope, and implications of data collection and use, affording individuals the opportunity to make informed decisions. This practice underscores the importance of respecting privacy.

7. **Responsible Vulnerability Disclosure:** Ethical cybersecurity professionals adhere to responsible vulnerability disclosure practices. Instead of exploiting vulnerabilities for personal gain or malicious purposes, they responsibly report them to affected parties or appropriate authorities, enabling timely mitigation and protection.

8. **Continuous Learning and Professional Development:** Ethical conduct encompasses a commitment to continuous learning and professional development. Professionals should remain updated with the latest technological advancements, emerging threats, and industry best practices to provide effective and knowledgeable cybersecurity services.

9. **Collaboration and Teamwork:** Ethical cybersecurity professionals actively engage in collaborative efforts and work in teams to address security challenges. They share knowledge, expertise, and resources while respecting the contributions and perspectives of others. This fosters a culture of teamwork and cooperation, strengthening the collective security posture.

10. **Ethical Decision-Making:** Professionals are expected to engage in ethical decision-making processes when confronted with complex situations or dilemmas. They should carefully consider the potential impact of their actions on individuals, organisations, and society. Ethical decision-making involves a comprehensive analysis of ethical considerations, a thorough assessment of risks, and a commitment to acting in accordance with moral principles.

5.3.2 Identify Unethical Conduct within Cybersecurity

Unethical conduct within the realm of cybersecurity encompasses actions that run counter to established ethical principles and professional standards. These behaviours compromise the integrity, privacy, and security of individuals, organisations, or systems. While the list provided is not exhaustive, it serves to illustrate examples of unethical conduct:

1. **Sabotage:** Engaging in activities with the deliberate intention of disrupting or causing damage to computer systems, networks, or data without proper authorisation is considered unethical. This includes executing denial-of-service (DoS) attacks, introducing destructive malware, or intentionally causing system failures, which can lead to significant disruptions and potential harm.

2. **Disclosure or Misuse of Confidential Information:** Unethical conduct involves the unauthorised disclosure, sale, or misuse of confidential information. This may entail leaking sensitive data, selling personal information on the black market, or exploiting privileged access to gain unauthorised benefits or harm others. Such actions compromise the trust and security associated with confidential information.

3. **Maliciously Injuring Reputation or Prospects:** Engaging in activities with the intent to harm the reputation, prospects, or operations of individuals, businesses, or organisations is considered unethical. This can include spreading false information, participating in online defamation or cyberbullying, or orchestrating malicious campaigns aimed at damaging an entity's reputation. Such conduct can have far-reaching consequences for the affected parties.

4. **Unauthorised Access and Intrusion:** Gaining unauthorized access to computer systems, networks, or accounts, which includes hacking into private systems without proper permission, is deemed unethical. Intruding into someone's personal or organisational space without legitimate authorisation not only violates privacy but also breaches trust, potentially leading to significant harm and loss of sensitive information.

5. **Cyber Espionage and Intellectual Property Theft:** Engaging in cyber espionage, which involves unauthorised access or theft of confidential information, trade secrets, or intellectual property, is considered unethical. Such actions not only harm businesses but also compromise innovation and violate legal rights, leading to severe consequences for the affected entities.

6. **Unauthorised Surveillance and Monitoring:** Illegally monitoring or spying on individuals or organisations without proper legal authorisation is unethical. This includes activities such as unauthorised wiretapping, intrusive surveillance, or using spyware to monitor someone's online activities without their knowledge or consent, infringing upon privacy rights and potentially causing harm or distress.

7. **Exploiting Vulnerabilities for Personal Gain:** Taking advantage of security vulnerabilities for personal gain, financial profit, or malicious intent is unethical. This may involve exploiting vulnerabilities for personal financial gain, engaging in ransomware attacks, or using stolen information for fraudulent activities, potentially leading to significant harm and financial loss.

8. **Cyberstalking and Online Harassment:** Engaging in persistent and targeted harassment, stalking, or threatening behaviour towards individuals online is considered unethical. This includes sending abusive messages, spreading personal information without consent, or engaging in online stalking with the intention of causing harm or distress, potentially leading to severe emotional and psychological repercussions.

9. **Unauthorised Alteration or Destruction of Data:** Unethical conduct involves unauthorised alteration, destruction, or manipulation of data, files, or systems. Intentionally modifying or deleting data without proper authorisation can have severe consequences, including financial loss, legal implications, and disruptions to operations, potentially causing significant harm to affected parties.

10. **Lack of Transparency and Disclosure:** Failing to be transparent and disclose relevant information to individuals or organisations when handling their data or conducting cybersecurity activities is considered unethical. This includes concealing security breaches, failing to inform affected parties, or deliberately misleading stakeholders about security practices, potentially leading to breaches of trust and legal repercussions.

Quiz: Ethical and unethical conduct within cybersecurity

1. Ethical or Unethical: A cybersecurity professional discovers a critical vulnerability in a widely used software application. Instead of disclosing it to the vendor, they exploit the vulnerability for personal gain.

    a) Ethical
    b) Unethical

2. Ethical or Unethical: An organisation's cybersecurity team conducts regular penetration tests and vulnerability assessments on their network to identify and remediate potential security weaknesses.

    a) Ethical
    b) Unethical

3. Ethical or Unethical: A cybersecurity consultant exaggerates the severity of security threats to persuade a client to purchase unnecessary cybersecurity products and services.

    a) Ethical b) Unethical

4. Ethical or Unethical: A cybersecurity researcher discovers a zero-day vulnerability in a widely used operating system. They promptly report the vulnerability to the vendor and work collaboratively to develop a patch before disclosing it publicly.

    a) Ethical b) Unethical

5. Ethical or Unethical: A cybersecurity analyst accesses confidential company data without proper authorisation to gather evidence for an ongoing investigation into a suspected insider threat.

    a) Ethical b) Unethical

6. Ethical or Unethical: A cybersecurity professional leaks sensitive customer data to the media to expose security flaws within their organisation, despite having signed a non-disclosure agreement.
    a) Ethical b) Unethical

7. Ethical or Unethical: A cybersecurity team conducts social engineering tests on employees without their knowledge or consent to assess their susceptibility to phishing attacks.
    a) Ethical b) Unethical

8. Ethical or Unethical: A cybersecurity manager provides comprehensive security training and resources to all employees to help them recognise and mitigate cybersecurity risks effectively.
    a) Ethical b) Unethical

9. Ethical or Unethical: A cybersecurity firm hires hackers to launch DDoS attacks on competitors' websites to gain a competitive advantage in the market.
    a) Ethical b) Unethical

10. Ethical or Unethical: A cybersecurity professional discloses security vulnerabilities discovered during an authorised penetration test to the affected organisation promptly, allowing them to address the issues before any exploitation occurs.
    a) Ethical b) Unethical

Chapter 6: Mastering Professional Skills in Cybersecurity

Learning Outcome:
- **6.1 Understand behaviours required for a career in cybersecurity.**
    - Explain the importance of managing and promoting a positive digital identity.
    - Describe possible employee screening checks that an employer might carry out.
    - Consider potential consequences of unsatisfactory findings because of employer checks.
    - Describe the following security clearance levels: • BPSS (Baseline Personnel Security Standard) • SC (Security Checked) • DV (Developed Vetting.
    - Explain how bias can influence cybersecurity.
    - Describe the benefits of a security by design mindset.
- **6.2 Be able to identify skills required for a career in cybersecurity.**
    - Identify skills required for a career in cybersecurity.
    - Perform a personal skills analysis.
    - Assess own skills against those required for a career in cybersecurity.
    - Create a personal development plan.
- **6.3 Understand the importance of continuous professional development.**
    - Explain the term continuous professional development (CPD).
    - State methods of keeping up to date with industry knowledge.
    - Explain why it is important to keep CPD up to date.

6. About this chapter

Chapter 6 invites you to embark on a transformative journey through the multifaceted landscape of cybersecurity, blending insights into professional skills and the art of personal development. Throughout this chapter, various quizzes serve as tutorial activities, engaging readers in active learning experiences.

Beginning with an in-depth exploration of the professional skills and behaviours essential for success in the cybersecurity domain, the chapter meticulously outlines technical proficiencies and soft skills imperative for navigating the complexities of this ever-evolving field. From technical competencies like programming languages and data analysis to crucial soft skills such as communication and problem-solving, readers gain a holistic understanding of the skill set demanded by the cybersecurity landscape.

Diving further, the chapter unfolds a comprehensive guide on performing a Personal Skills Analysis. Readers are equipped with a strategic roadmap to identify their purpose, evaluate existing skills through self-reflection, and objectively assess strengths and weaknesses. The chapter advocates for soliciting diverse feedback, prioritising skills based on relevance, and crafting actionable plans, reinforcing the importance of continuous improvement.

Delving into strategic planning tools, the chapter distinctively compares SWOT and SOAR analysis, providing nuanced perspectives on how these methodologies can shape cybersecurity strategies. It is a critical exploration that adds layers of depth to understanding and navigating cybersecurity terrain.

The narrative then seamlessly transitions into an actionable assessment of personal skills against the dynamic requisites of a cybersecurity career. By reviewing job descriptions, identifying core competencies, and seeking feedback, readers gain a profound understanding of how to strategically bridge skill gaps through education, training, and practical experience.

The journey culminates in crafting a Personal Development Plan, a roadmap adorned with SMART goals, ushering readers towards their professional aspirations. The chapter concludes by emphasizing the pivotal role of Continuous Professional Development (CPD), illuminating key principles, benefits, and methods for staying abreast of industry knowledge.

Designed for both novices and seasoned professionals, Chapter 6 stands as a beacon, guiding readers through the intricate interplay of professional skills, personal development, and the ever-evolving landscape of cybersecurity. It is an indispensable resource for those committed to not only navigating but excelling in the dynamic world of cybersecurity.

6.1 Understand behaviours required for a career in cybersecurity.

In the realm of cybersecurity, the fusion of professional skills and behaviours is paramount to safeguarding computer systems, networks, and data from the ever-evolving landscape of cyber threats. Below are detailed descriptions of key skills and behaviours that hold substantial value in the cybersecurity profession:

1. **Problem-Solving**

    1. Cybersecurity professionals are often faced with intricate challenges demanding analytical prowess and critical thinking skills.
    2. They must excel at identifying vulnerabilities, delving into security incidents, and conceiving innovative solutions to fortify systems and protect invaluable data.

2. **Technical Knowledge**

    1. A solid foundation in technical expertise is indispensable for cybersecurity practitioners.
    2. This encompasses an in-depth understanding of networking protocols, proficiency in operating systems, proficiency in programming languages, mastery of encryption techniques, and familiarity with a spectrum of security technologies and tools.

3. **Communication**

    1. Effective communication skills are pivotal for cybersecurity professionals.
    2. They must possess the ability to articulate complex technical concepts in a clear and understandable manner to non-technical stakeholders. Additionally, they need to collaborate seamlessly with colleagues and proficiently communicate security risks and recommendations to management.

4. **Threat Intelligence**

    1. Remaining abreast of the latest cyber threats and attack methodologies is imperative.
    2. Cybersecurity professionals are tasked with the continuous monitoring and analysis of emerging threats, vulnerabilities, and exploits. This enables them to anticipate potential risks and proactively take measures to mitigate them.

5. **Ethical Conduct**
    1. Demonstrating an unwavering commitment to ethics and integrity is non-negotiable for cybersecurity professionals.
    2. Given their privileged access to sensitive information and systems, they are held to the highest standards of confidentiality and privacy.

6. **Continuous Learning**
    1. The cybersecurity landscape is in a perpetual state of flux, demanding ongoing learning and adaptation.
    2. Professionals must actively engage in certifications, industry conferences, training programs, and relentless pursuit of new knowledge to remain at the forefront of emerging threats and technologies.

7. **Attention to Detail**
    1. A meticulous eye for detail is a hallmark of cybersecurity professionals.
    2. They must methodically scrutinise systems, logs, and data, keenly attuned to identifying potential security vulnerabilities and any irregularities that may signal a breach or suspicious activity.

8. **Collaboration**
    1. Cybersecurity is a collaborative endeavour, necessitating adeptness in working harmoniously with colleagues across different teams and departments.
    2. This collaborative spirit is vital for the development of comprehensive security strategies and for an effective response to incidents.

9. **Adaptability**
    1. The cybersecurity landscape is marked by dynamic shifts and constant evolution.
    2. Professionals must exhibit a nimble ability to adapt swiftly to new challenges and emerging technologies. They should thrive in high-pressure scenarios and make informed decisions under tight timelines.

10. **Risk Management**
    1. A comprehensive grasp of risk and the application of judicious risk management strategies are pivotal in cybersecurity.

2. Professionals must be adept at assessing vulnerabilities, gauging potential impacts, and implementing controls to mitigate risks effectively.

It is important to emphasize that while this list provides a comprehensive overview, the specific skills and behaviours required may vary based on the organisation, job role, and specialisation within cybersecurity. Nevertheless, possessing these fundamental skills and behaviours serves as a cornerstone for success in the dynamic and critical field of cybersecurity.

Tutorial Activity – General Quiz

1. What are some fundamental skills and behaviours important for success in a professional career such as cybersecurity?
2. Why is problem-solving considered an essential skill in various professions?
3. Discuss the significance of technical knowledge in today's job market.
4. How does effective communication contribute to workplace success?
5. Why is staying updated on industry trends and advancements important for professionals?
6. Explain the importance of ethical conduct in any professional setting.
7. How can continuous learning benefit individuals in their careers?
8. What role does attention to detail play in ensuring quality work?
9. Why is collaboration emphasized as a valuable skill in teamwork environments?
10. Discuss the importance of adaptability in navigating changes and challenges in the workplace.
11. What is risk management, and why is it relevant in the context of cybersecurity professions?

6.1.1 Importance of Managing and Promoting a Positive Digital Identity

In today's interconnected world, the significance of managing and promoting a positive digital identity cannot be overstated. It encompasses a range of crucial aspects that profoundly impact both personal and professional spheres. Here are detailed explanations of why it holds such paramount importance:

1. **Reputation**
    1. Your digital identity serves as a mirror reflecting how you are perceived in the online realm. It wields significant influence in shaping your reputation, both on a personal and professional level. Employers, colleagues, clients, and potential partners often turn to online sources to form impressions about individuals. An actively managed and positively promoted digital identity aids in constructing a favourable reputation, fostering trust, and enhancing overall credibility.

2. **Professional Opportunities**
    1. A positive digital identity acts as a gateway to a myriad of professional prospects. Employers frequently engage in online research when evaluating job applicants, and a negative online presence can adversely affect your chances of securing coveted positions. Conversely, a meticulously managed digital identity that highlights your skills, achievements, and professionalism amplifies your potential for career progression, networking, and accessing new opportunities.

3. **Personal Branding**
    1. Consider your digital identity as an extension of your personal brand. It affords you the ability to sculpt and regulate the narrative surrounding your interests, values, and expertise. Through conscious management and promotion of a positive digital identity, you can harmonise your online presence with your personal objectives, principles, and aspirations.

4. **Online Safety**
    1. A positive digital identity substantially contributes to your online safety and security. By exercising prudence in what you share online, fortifying your privacy settings, and thoughtfully managing your virtual interactions, you diminish the risk of falling victim to identity theft, cyberbullying, and other nefarious activities. Promoting a positive digital identity serves as a deterrent to attracting negative attention and potential threats.

5. **Digital Footprint**
    1. Every action taken online leaves behind a trace, forming what is known as a digital footprint. Skilful management and promotion of a positive digital identity afford you control over this footprint. This involves a mindful approach to the content you generate and share, as well as the associations

you forge online. A positive digital footprint yields enduring effects, while rectifying a negative one can prove to be a formidable challenge.

6. **Networking and Collaboration**
    1. A positive digital identity serves as an invaluable catalyst for networking and collaboration. It empowers you to connect with kindred spirits, industry experts, and professionals in your field. Through active management and promotion of your digital identity, you can partake in substantive dialogues, disseminate knowledge, and construct meaningful relationships within online communities.

7. **Digital Citizenship**
    1. Cultivating and nurturing a positive digital identity forms an integral facet of being a responsible digital citizen. This entails adhering to ethical tenets, respecting the privacy and intellectual property rights of others, and contributing constructively to online communities. By curating a positive digital identity, you make a meaningful contribution to cultivating a healthier and more constructive online environment for all.

The meticulous management and promotion of a positive digital identity reverberates through various aspects of our lives, from professional growth and networking to personal branding and online safety. It is a cornerstone of responsible digital citizenship in an interconnected world.

Tutorial Activity - Multiple-choice Quiz

These questions aim to test understanding of the importance and implications of managing and promoting a positive digital identity as discussed in this section:

1. What is one significant aspect impacted by managing and promoting a positive digital identity?
    a) Physical health
    b) Professional reputation
    c) Spiritual well-being
    d) Fashion sense?

2. How does a positive digital identity contribute to professional opportunities?
    a) It increases online shopping options.
    b) It enhances job security.

       c) It decreases networking capabilities.
       d) It amplifies career prospects.

3. Which of the following best describes the concept of a digital footprint?
    a) The physical evidence of outdoor activities
    b) The trace left behind by online activities
    c) A virtual shoe worn for online interaction
    d) The measurable impact of digital marketing campaigns?

4. How does managing and promoting a positive digital identity contribute to online safety?
    a) By increasing the likelihood of winning online contests
    b) By attracting negative attention and potential threats
    c) By reducing the risk of identity theft and cyberbullying
    d) By making one more susceptible to online scams?

5. What role does a positive digital identity play in networking and collaboration?
    a) It serves as a barrier to forming meaningful relationships.
    b) It limits the potential for industry engagement.
    c) It fosters connections with professionals and experts.
    d) It isolates individuals from online communities.

6.1.2 Employee Screening Checks that an Employer Might Carry Out

When employers embark on the process of hiring new personnel, it is imperative that they conduct various screening checks to make well-informed decisions and mitigate potential risks. These checks serve to ensure that candidates meet the requisite criteria and align with the values and requirements of the organisation. Here are comprehensive explanations of some of the most common employee screening checks that employers might carry out:

1. **Background Checks**

    Background checks are instrumental in validating the accuracy of information provided by candidates. This encompasses a thorough examination of employment history, educational qualifications, professional licenses, and certifications. Furthermore, employers may opt to conduct criminal background checks to ascertain any prior criminal records that may be relevant to the role. This multifaceted process allows employers to build a comprehensive understanding of a candidate's professional and legal background.

2. **Reference Checks**

    Reference checks serve as a pivotal step in the screening process. This involves reaching out to the references provided by the candidate to glean insights into their past work performance, skills, and character. By engaging with previous supervisors or colleagues, employers gain valuable perspectives that aid in assessing the candidate's suitability for the role. Additionally, reference checks serve to corroborate the information furnished by the candidate in their application.

3. **Identity Verification**

    Ensuring that a candidate's identity aligns with the information provided is essential. Employers may undertake identity verification by scrutinising official identification documents, such as passports or driver's licenses. This meticulous process allows employers to confirm the authenticity of a candidate's identity and ensures they are indeed who they claim to be.

4. **Drug and Alcohol Screening**

    In certain industries, especially those where safety is paramount, employers may implement drug and alcohol screening tests. This is particularly relevant for positions where substance abuse could pose risks to the well-being of employees or customers. By conducting these tests, employers aim to create a safe and secure work environment while minimising potential risks associated with substance use.

5. **Credit Checks**

    For roles that involve financial responsibilities, employers may opt to conduct credit checks. This involves a thorough examination of a candidate's financial history, encompassing credit scores, payment records, and outstanding debts. By conducting credit checks, employers gain insights into a candidate's financial responsibility and integrity, which is particularly pertinent for positions where fiduciary duties are involved.

6. **Social Media Screening**

    Employers may choose to review a candidate's social media profiles as part of their screening process. This practice provides employers with a window into a candidate's online behaviour, professionalism, and alignment with the values of the organisation. However, it is crucial for employers to conduct social media screening ethically and within the bounds of legal boundaries, respecting privacy rights and avoiding discriminatory practices.

7. **Professional License and Certification Verification**

    Positions that require specific licenses or certifications necessitate diligent verification of the authenticity and validity of those credentials. This step ensures that candidates possess the necessary qualifications and professional standing required to excel in their designated roles.

Disclosure and Barring Service (DBS)

The Disclosure and Barring Service (DBS) check in the UK is an integral process for evaluating an individual's criminal background in the context of specific roles. This encompasses information about convictions, cautions, and warnings. The three tiers of checks include basic, standard, and enhanced. The basic check reveals unspent convictions, while the standard and enhanced checks provide more comprehensive insights. The application process involves the completion of a form and submission of identification documents. The resulting DBS certificate serves to transparently communicate an individual's criminal history to potential employers or organizations. By facilitating this check, vulnerable groups are safeguarded, and employers are equipped to make judicious decisions regarding an individual's suitability for particular roles. This process underscores the commitment to creating safe and secure environments for all stakeholders involved.

Tutorial Activity - Multiple-choice Quiz

These questions aim to assess understanding of the various employee screening checks employers might carry out during the hiring process:
1. What is the purpose of conducting background checks during the hiring process?
    a) To assess a candidate's social media activity
    b) To verify the accuracy of information provided by candidates

c) To evaluate a candidate's financial history
   d) To determine a candidate's preferred work hours

2. What information do reference checks aim to provide about a candidate?
   a) Their favourite hobbies and interests
   b) Their personal social media handles
   c) Insights into their past work performance and character
   d) Their preferred mode of transportation to work

3. Why might employers implement drug and alcohol screening tests during the hiring process?
   a) To ensure candidates are physically fit for the job
   b) To assess candidates' social media activity
   c) To create a safe work environment and minimise risks associated with substance abuse
   d) To evaluate candidates' financial responsibility

4. In what circumstances might employers conduct credit checks during the hiring process?
   a) For positions requiring specific licenses or certifications
   b) For roles involving financial responsibilities
   c) For roles with a heavy focus on social media engagement
   d) For positions requiring physical fitness assessments

5. What is the purpose of the Disclosure and Barring Service (DBS) check in the UK?
   a) To evaluate a candidate's credit history
   b) To verify a candidate's educational qualifications
   c) To assess a candidate's proficiency in specific software programs
   d) To evaluate an individual's criminal background in the context of certain roles

6.1.3 Consequences of Unsatisfactory Findings as a Result of Employer Checks

When unsatisfactory findings emerge from employer checks, it initiates a chain of potential consequences that reverberate through both the employer's operations and the candidate's prospects. Here, we delve into the detailed ramifications that can unfold:

1. **Disqualification from the Hiring Process**

    In light of unsatisfactory findings, the employer may opt to disqualify the candidate from further consideration for the position. This pivotal decision essentially closes the door on the candidate's opportunity to secure the job. It marks a critical juncture in the candidate's professional journey, potentially altering their career trajectory.

2. **Damage to Reputation**

    For candidates, unsatisfactory findings can wield a detrimental impact on their professional reputation and credibility. The revelation of negative information pertaining to their employment history, educational background, or criminal record can cast a shadow on their suitability for future job opportunities. This erosion of reputation can be a formidable hurdle to overcome.

3. **Legal and Compliance Issues**

    Employers must tread carefully through the legal and compliance landscape when conducting screening checks. Failing to adhere to proper procedures or conducting checks in a discriminatory or unlawful manner can plunge the employer into a legal quagmire. This may entail potential lawsuits for violating privacy, anti-discrimination, or employment laws, incurring significant legal ramifications.

4. **Trust and Integrity Concerns**

    Unsatisfactory findings have the potential to raise profound concerns about a candidate's trustworthiness and integrity. This can sow seeds of doubt in the employer's mind regarding the candidate's ability to perform the job effectively, particularly in roles necessitating high levels of trust, confidentiality, or financial responsibility. This erosion of trust can fundamentally alter the dynamics of the hiring decision.

5. **Reputational Damage for Employers**

    Employers risk incurring reputational damage if it comes to light that they failed to adequately screen candidates or employed individuals with questionable backgrounds or qualifications. This can wield far-reaching consequences, impacting the credibility of the organisation, tarnishing its brand image, and potentially straining relationships with stakeholders, including customers, clients, and business partners.

6. **Increased Hiring Costs**

    Should unsatisfactory findings lead to the disqualification of candidates late in the hiring process, it can precipitate increased costs for the employer. This encompasses expenses related to rebooting the recruitment process, conducting additional screening checks on new candidates, and potentially delaying the onboarding and subsequent productivity of the chosen candidate. These increased costs can strain the organisation's budgetary resources.

7. **Employee Performance and Trust Issues**

    Should unsatisfactory findings surface after a candidate has been hired, it can introduce performance and trust issues within the organisation. Employers may find themselves grappling with concerns related to competency, credibility, or potential risks associated with the employee's background. This can lead to disruptions in team dynamics, hindered productivity, and necessitate a recalibration of the working relationship.

The discovery of unsatisfactory findings because of employer checks sets in motion a cascade of consequences that impact both the employer and the candidate. It underscores the critical importance of diligent and ethical screening practices in safeguarding the interests of all parties involved in the hiring process.

Tutorial Activity - Multiple-choice Quiz

These questions aim to assess understanding of the consequences that may arise from unsatisfactory findings because of employer checks during the hiring process:

1. What is one potential consequence for a candidate resulting from unsatisfactory findings during employer checks?
   a) Promotion within the organisation
   b) Disqualification from the hiring process
   c) Salary negotiation opportunities
   d) Increased networking prospects?

2. How might unsatisfactory findings impact a candidate's professional reputation?
   a) They may lead to increased job offers.
   b) They could enhance credibility in the industry.
   c) They may cast doubt on suitability for future job opportunities.
   d) They could lead to rapid career advancement.

3. What legal risks might employers face if they fail to conduct screening checks properly?
   a) Reduced employee turnover
   b) Enhanced brand recognition
   c) Potential lawsuits for violating privacy or employment laws
   d) Improved customer satisfaction

4. What concerns may arise for employers regarding a candidate's trustworthiness and integrity?
   a) Heightened employee morale
   b) Increased team collaboration
   c) Doubts about the candidate's ability to perform the job effectively
   d) Enhanced organisational culture

5. How might the discovery of unsatisfactory findings impact an employer's reputation?
   a) It may lead to increased trust among stakeholders.
   b) It could improve relationships with clients and partners.
   c) It may result in reputational damage and tarnish the organisation's brand image.
   d) It could enhance employee engagement levels

6.1.4 Security Clearance Levels

Security clearances are crucial for granting individuals access to sensitive information and projects. They vary in scope and intensity, tailored to specific roles and the level of classified information involved. Here are detailed descriptions of three prominent security clearance levels in the United Kingdom:

1. **BPSS (Baseline Personnel Security Standard)**

   The BPSS clearance serves as an entry-level security clearance in the United Kingdom. It is designed to establish a foundational level of security assurance for individuals who will be handling non-critical or non-sensitive roles, particularly in the context of government contracts or access to sensitive government information. The BPSS clearance encompasses basic checks, including verification of identity, scrutiny of employment history, and examination of any criminal records. It acts as a baseline measure to ensure a minimum level of trustworthiness in handling less sensitive information.

2. **SC (Security Checked)**

   SC clearance represents a higher level of security clearance in the UK. It is geared towards individuals who will be handling information of greater sensitivity or working on projects deemed crucial to national security. The SC clearance involves a more extensive background check compared to the BPSS clearance. This includes a thorough evaluation of an individual's personal and professional history, financial situation, and any relevant criminal record. The SC clearance is pivotal for roles where access to sensitive information is paramount, ensuring a heightened level of trustworthiness and reliability.

3. **DV (Developed Vetting)**

   DV clearance stands as the pinnacle of security clearances in the UK. It is reserved for individuals who will have access to the highest levels of classified information or will be engaged in activities of utmost significance to national security. The DV clearance process is the most exhaustive and intrusive, entailing a comprehensive background investigation. This encompasses a detailed examination of an individual's personal, financial, and social background. The vetting process may incorporate interviews, character references, and extensive scrutiny of family, associates, and foreign contacts. The stringent nature of DV clearance ensures an unparalleled level of trust and reliability for individuals with access to the most sensitive information.

It is paramount to acknowledge that security clearance levels, along with their specific criteria and processes, may vary substantially across different countries and organisations.

While the descriptions provided offer a general overview of the three security clearance levels outlined, the actual requirements and procedures may entail more comprehensive and tailored assessments in practice. This underscores the critical nature of aligning security clearances with the unique demands of each role and the sensitivity of the information involved.

Tutorial Activity - Multiple-choice Quiz

These questions aim to assess understanding of the different security clearance levels outlined in the section and their purposes:

1. Which security clearance level serves as an entry-level clearance in the United Kingdom?
   a) SC (Security Checked)
   b) DV (Developed Vetting)
   c) BPSS (Baseline Personnel Security Standard)
   d) Top Secret Clearance

2. What is the purpose of the BPSS clearance?
   a) Granting access to the highest levels of classified information
   b) Establishing a foundational level of security assurance
   c) Conducting thorough financial investigations
   d) Performing detailed interviews with foreign contacts

3. Which security clearance level is crucial for roles involving access to sensitive government information?
   a) SC (Security Checked)
   b) DV (Developed Vetting)
   c) BPSS (Baseline Personnel Security Standard)
   d) Confidential Clearance

4. What distinguishes the DV clearance from the SC clearance?
   a) The DV clearance involves basic checks, while the SC clearance is more extensive.
   b) The DV clearance is reserved for non-sensitive roles, while the SC clearance is for national security.
   c) The DV clearance requires a comprehensive background investigation, while the SC clearance involves only identity verification.
   d) The DV clearance is the entry-level clearance, while the SC clearance is the highest level.

5. Why is it important for security clearance levels to be aligned with the unique demands of each role?
   a) To make the clearance process faster
   b) To ensure a minimum level of trustworthiness
   c) To enhance the complexity of background checks
   d) To tailor the level of clearance to the sensitivity of the information involved.

6.1.5 How Bias Can Influence Cybersecurity

The influence of bias in cybersecurity is far-reaching and can significantly impact various facets of security practices and outcomes. Below are nuanced ways in which bias manifests and shapes cybersecurity efforts:

1. **Risk Assessment and Threat Modelling**

   Bias can sway how organisations perceive and prioritise risks in cybersecurity. Preconceived notions, unconscious biases, or stereotypes may lead to the underestimation or overestimation of specific threats. This skewed risk assessment can result in a misallocation of resources, with some areas receiving inadequate protection while others may be overly emphasized, ultimately leading to vulnerabilities and gaps in the overall security posture.

2. **Security Design and Implementation**

   The design and implementation of security systems, protocols, and technologies can be significantly influenced by bias. If the individuals involved in this process hold biased beliefs or assumptions, it can impact the efficacy and inclusivity of the security measures. For instance, biased assumptions about user behaviours or demographics may lead to security controls that unintentionally discriminate against certain user groups or fail to adequately protect them, creating potential security blind spots.

3. **Data Collection and Analysis**

   Bias in data collection and analysis can have a profound impact on the accuracy and efficacy of cybersecurity strategies. Biased data collection methods or the exclusion of specific demographics can result in incomplete or skewed datasets. This, in turn, can lead to biased conclusions, suboptimal threat detection, and ineffective decision-making in the realm of cybersecurity operations.

4. **Hiring and Workforce Diversity**

   Bias can permeate the composition of cybersecurity teams. If biased hiring practices persist, it may lead to a lack of diversity within the cybersecurity workforce. This absence of diverse perspectives can hinder innovation, limit problem-solving approaches, and create potential blind spots in understanding and mitigating security threats effectively.

5. **Incident Response and Investigation**

   Bias can exert an influence on incident response and investigation processes. If biases exist among cybersecurity professionals, it may lead to premature assumptions or conclusions based on limited information. This can result in misattribution or misclassification of security incidents, potentially delaying the appropriate response or overlooking critical evidence that could be instrumental in resolving the incident.

6. **User Experience and Usability**

   Bias can also shape the user experience and usability of cybersecurity systems and applications. Biased assumptions about user behaviour or familiarity with technology can lead to the creation of complex or confusing security controls. This can inadvertently prompt users to bypass security measures or make errors that compromise the overall security of the system.

Recognising and mitigating bias within cybersecurity is crucial to ensuring that security practices are fair, effective, and inclusive. By addressing bias, organisations can enhance their overall security posture and better protect against evolving cyber threats.

Tutorial Activity - Multiple-choice Quiz

These questions aim to assess understanding of how bias can influence various aspects of cybersecurity practices and outcomes:

1. How can bias influence risk assessment and threat modelling in cybersecurity?
   a) It leads to an underestimation of all threats.
   b) It results in an overemphasis on specific threats.
   c) It ensures an equal distribution of resources across all potential threats.
   d) It has no impact on risk assessment practices.

2. In what way can bias affect the design and implementation of security systems?
   a) It ensures inclusivity in security measures.
   b) It leads to unbiased assumptions about user behaviours.
   c) It may result in security controls that unintentionally discriminate against certain user groups.
   d) It guarantees the effectiveness of security protocols.

3. How does bias in data collection and analysis impact cybersecurity strategies?
   a) It enhances threat detection capabilities.
   b) It leads to biased conclusions and suboptimal threat detection.
   c) It ensures the completeness of datasets.
   d) It has no impact on decision-making in cybersecurity operations.

4. What potential consequences can bias hiring practices have on cybersecurity teams?
   a) Increased diversity of perspectives and problem-solving approaches.
   b) Limitations in understanding and mitigating security threats effectively.
   c) Improved innovation and teamwork.
   d) Enhanced recruitment processes.

5. How might bias influence incident response and investigation processes?
   a) It ensures accurate conclusions based on limited information.
   b) It leads to a faster resolution of security incidents.
   c) It may result in premature assumptions or misclassification of security incidents.
   d) It has no impact on incident response procedures.

6.1.6 Benefits of a Security by Design Mindset

A security by design mindset is a holistic approach that embeds security considerations into every phase of the development lifecycle, from initial conception to implementation and ongoing maintenance. This approach yields a host of valuable advantages:

1. **Proactive Risk Mitigation**

   Early integration of security enables the identification and mitigation of potential vulnerabilities and risks at their inception. This proactive approach significantly reduces the likelihood of security breaches and minimises the potential damage that could be inflicted.

2. **Cost Savings**

   Incorporating security measures during the design phase proves to be more cost-effective compared to retrofitting security post-development. Rectifying security flaws at later stages or after deployment tends to be more time-consuming, resource-intensive, and financially burdensome.

3. **Enhanced Security and Privacy**

   A security by design approach results in fortified security and privacy measures. It guarantees the proper implementation of security controls, robust encryption protocols, stringent access management, and robust data protection mechanisms. This, in turn, diminishes the likelihood of unauthorised access, data breaches, or privacy violations.

4. **Improved User Trust**

   Embracing security by design showcases a dedication to safeguarding user data and privacy. This cultivates trust among users, customers, and stakeholders, as it demonstrates that their information is safeguarded, thereby instilling greater confidence in the system or application.

5. **Compliance with Regulations**

   Numerous industries impose specific regulatory mandates pertaining to data protection and security. Embracing a security by design ethos streamlines compliance with these regulations, thereby averting potential legal and financial repercussions associated with non-compliance.

6. **Faster Response to Emerging Threats**

   A security by design mindset fosters an environment of continuous monitoring and adaptability in the face of evolving security threats. This empowers organisations to respond swiftly to emerging vulnerabilities or attacks, facilitating prompt deployment of updates, patches, and remediation measures.

7. **Stronger Resilience**

    Infusing security into the design phase bolsters the resilience of systems and applications. By considering potential risks and threats during development, organisations can architect robust frameworks and implement measures that withstand attacks, minimise the impact of breaches, and facilitate swift recovery.

8. **Competitive Advantage**

    In today's security-conscious landscape, organisations that prioritise security by design gain a distinct competitive edge. Demonstrating a steadfast commitment to security can be a differentiating factor, drawing in customers who prioritise data protection and privacy.

A security by design mindset is indispensable for crafting robust and resilient systems and applications. By integrating security throughout the development process, organisations can achieve heightened protection against threats, establish user trust, adhere to regulations, and mitigate potential risks, resulting in safer and more dependable products and services.

Tutorial Activity - Multiple-choice Quiz

These questions aim to assess understanding of the benefits associated with adopting a security by design mindset in cybersecurity practices:

1. What is one benefit of adopting a security by design mindset?
    a) Reactive risk mitigation
    b) Increased likelihood of security breaches
    c) Proactive risk mitigation
    d) Higher cost of security implementation

2. How does incorporating security measures during the design phase affect costs compared to retrofitting security post-development?
    a) It increases costs significantly.
    b) It has no impact on costs.
    c) It is more cost-effective.
    d) It reduces the quality of security measures.

3. What is one advantage of embracing security by design in terms of user trust?
   a) Decreased confidence in the system or application
   b) Higher likelihood of data breaches
   c) Enhanced user trust due to safeguarding of data and privacy
   d) Increased scepticism among stakeholders

4. How does a security by design approach contribute to compliance with regulations?
   a) It increases the risk of legal and financial repercussions.
   b) It has no impact on regulatory compliance.
   c) It streamlines compliance with regulations.
   d) It leads to non-compliance with regulatory mandates.

5. What advantage does a security by design mindset offer in responding to emerging threats?
   a) It delays the response to emerging threats.
   b) It minimises the need for updates and patches.
   c) It fosters an environment of continuous monitoring and adaptability.
   d) It leads to slower deployment of remediation measures.

6.2.1 Skills Required for a Career in Cybersecurity

A successful career in cybersecurity demands a diverse skill set to proficiently safeguard computer systems, networks, and data against a spectrum of security threats. Here are the fundamental skills essential for a career in cybersecurity:

1. **Technical Proficiency**

   A robust comprehension of computer systems, networks, operating systems, and programming languages forms the bedrock of cybersecurity expertise. Proficiency in cybersecurity tools, techniques, and protocols is pivotal for identifying vulnerabilities, deploying security measures, and mounting effective responses to security incidents.

2. **Information Security Mastery**

   Command over information security principles, industry standards, and best practices is paramount. This encompasses a grasp of concepts like risk management, access control, encryption, authentication, and secure coding practices.

3. **Network Security Competence**

   A thorough grasp of network architecture, protocols, and security technologies is critical for fortifying networks against unauthorized access, intrusions, and data breaches. Proficiency in firewalls, intrusion detection and prevention systems, virtual private networks (VPNs), and network monitoring is indispensable.

4. **Security Assessments and Testing Proficiency**

   The ability to execute security assessments and penetration testing to pinpoint vulnerabilities and weaknesses in systems is pivotal. Familiarity with tools and methodologies employed in ethical hacking and vulnerability scanning is requisite for evaluating and enhancing system security.

5. **Incident Response and Forensics Acumen**

   The capacity to adeptly respond to security incidents, probe breaches, and conduct digital forensics is crucial. This involves understanding incident response protocols, evidence collection and preservation, and proficiency in scrutinising security logs and system artifacts.

6. **Risk Management Expertise**

   Familiarity with risk assessment methodologies and the capability to evaluate and mitigate risks is imperative. Grasping concepts like business impact analysis, threat modelling, and the formulation of risk management strategies are indispensable skills.

7. **Security Governance and Compliance Proficiency**

   A sound grasp of security policies, regulatory requisites, and compliance frameworks is vital. Proficiency in crafting and implementing security policies, conducting audits, and ensuring organisational compliance bestows significant value.

8. **Communication and Collaboration Skill**

Effective communication and collaborative skills are pivotal in the realm of cybersecurity. The ability to convey intricate technical concepts to non-technical stakeholders, function as an integral part of a team, and collaborate with diverse departments are pivotal for triumph in this domain.

9. **Continuous Learning and Adaptability**

    Cybersecurity stands as a domain in perpetual flux, underscoring the necessity for an unwavering commitment to continuous learning. Staying abreast of the latest threats, technologies, and industry trends is crucial. Furthermore, the capacity to adeptly navigate new challenges and acquire new skills is of paramount importance.

10. **Ethical and Legal Acumen**

    A profound comprehension of ethical and legal parameters is pivotal in cybersecurity. Understanding the bounds of ethical hacking, familiarising oneself with privacy laws, and adhering to ethical guidelines and regulations are indispensable in this sphere.

It's imperative to recognise that this roster is not exhaustive. The specific skills requisite may vary contingent on the role and specialisation within the cybersecurity domain. Additionally, possessing problem-solving acumen, meticulous attention to detail, and a fervent spirit of inquiry are invaluable attributes in this domain.

Tutorial Activity - Multiple-choice Quiz

These 5 questions cover various skills and attributes required for a successful career in cybersecurity:
1. Question: What forms the foundational knowledge in cybersecurity, encompassing comprehension of computer systems, networks, and programming languages?
    1. a) Information Security Mastery
    2. b) Network Security Competence
    3. c) Technical Proficiency
    4. d) Security Assessments and Testing Proficiency
2. Question: What skill in cybersecurity involves understanding incident response protocols, evidence collection, and digital forensics?

1.
   1. a) Incident Response and Forensics Acumen
   2. b) Risk Management Expertise
   3. c) Security Governance and Compliance Proficiency
   4. d) Communication and Collaboration Skill

3. Question: What expertise in cybersecurity is vital for evaluating and mitigating risks, including concepts like business impact analysis and threat modelling?
   1. a) Continuous Learning and Adaptability
   2. b) Security Governance and Compliance Proficiency
   3. c) Risk Management Expertise
   4. d) Ethical and Legal Acumen

4. Question: Which skill in cybersecurity focuses on effective communication with non-technical stakeholders and collaboration within diverse departments?
   1. a) Technical Proficiency
   2. b) Communication and Collaboration Skill
   3. c) Incident Response and Forensics Acumen
   4. d) Security Assessments and Testing Proficiency

5. Question: What is essential for success in the dynamic field of cybersecurity, emphasizing continuous learning, and adaptability to new challenges and technologies?
   1. a) Ethical and Legal Acumen
   2. b) Technical Proficiency
   3. c) Continuous Learning and Adaptability
   4. d) Information Security Mastery

6.2.2 Performing a Personal Skills Analysis

Conducting a personal skills analysis is a crucial step in understanding one's strengths, weaknesses, and areas for growth. Below is a detailed guide on how to perform a personal skills analysis:

1. **Identify the Purpose**

   Clearly define the purpose of conducting a skills analysis. Are you aiming for a career transition, seeking professional development, or looking to enhance your current job performance? Understanding the underlying purpose will provide direction and focus for your analysis.

2. **Create a Comprehensive Skills List**

   Begin by compiling an exhaustive list of skills relevant to your target career or area of interest. This list should encompass both technical proficiencies and soft skills. Technical skills might encompass programming languages, data analysis, or project management, while soft skills could include communication, problem-solving, or leadership.

3. **Engage in Self-Reflection**

   Dedicate time to self-reflection to evaluate your existing skill set. Review your educational background, work experiences, and personal accomplishments. Consider both your professional and personal life to recognise skills acquired through diverse experiences.

4. **Evaluate Strengths and Weaknesses**

   Assess each skill on your list and gauge your proficiency level objectively. Be candid and impartial in appraising both your strengths and areas needing improvement. Additionally, seek feedback from colleagues, supervisors, or mentors to gain diverse perspectives.

5. **Prioritise Skills**

   After identifying your strengths and weaknesses, prioritise them based on their relevance and significance to your objectives. Concentrate on leveraging your strengths and identify areas for improvement that will yield the most substantial impact.

6. **Solicit Feedback**

   Seek input from individuals who have observed your skills in action. Their insights may shed light on aspects you might have overlooked. Colleagues, mentors, supervisors, and even friends or family members can provide valuable feedback.

7. **Spot Skill Gaps**

   Compare the skills you've pinpointed with the requisites of your target career or objectives. Recognise any disparities between your current skill set and what is demanded. This will enable you to discern which skills necessitate further refinement.

8. **Craft an Action Plan**

   Based on the identified skill gaps, formulate an action plan for enhancing and developing those skills. Establish Specific, Measurable, Achievable, Relevant, and Time-bound (SMART) objectives for each skill. Identify resources, courses, training programs, or professional development opportunities that can facilitate skill acquisition or enhancement.

9. **Implementation and Evaluation**

   Put your action plan into motion and initiate the process of acquiring new skills or refining existing ones. Monitor your progress, assess your performance, and adjust as necessary. Routinely reevaluate your skills to keep pace with your personal and professional advancement.

10. **Embrace Continuous Improvement**

    Remember that personal skills analysis is an ongoing endeavour. Continuously reassess your skills as you accrue experience and pursue fresh opportunities. Regularly revise and adapt your skills analysis to mirror your evolving goals and aspirations.

A meticulous personal skills analysis empowers individuals to make informed decisions about their career trajectories and professional growth. By understanding one's strengths and areas needing development, individuals can strategically shape their career paths.

6.2.3 Differentiate between SWOT and SOAR analysis

SWOT Analysis and SOAR Analysis are both invaluable tools for strategic planning, offering distinct approaches to assessing an organisation's current state and charting a course for the future. Here's an in-depth exploration of each:

SWOT Analysis

Strengths
- This component involves identifying and capitalising on internal positive attributes and advantages. These could encompass specialised expertise, unique capabilities, or abundant resources. Recognising strengths allows organisations/individuals to leverage them for competitive advantage.

Weaknesses
- Here, the focus is on evaluating internal areas that require improvement or where the organisation/individual may lag behind competitors. This could involve shortcomings such as skill gaps, limited resources, or inefficient processes. Identifying weaknesses enables targeted efforts for enhancement.

Opportunities
- This aspect revolves around recognising external factors or trends that can be advantageous for the organisation/individual. These could be emerging markets, technological advancements, evolving consumer needs, or untapped growth prospects. Taking opportunities involves aligning strategies to harness these trends.

Threats
- In this segment, organisations/individuals assess external challenges that have the potential to harm them. These may include factors like intense competition, economic downturns, regulatory shifts, or the entry of new market players. Identifying threats allows organisations to proactively prepare and mitigate risks.

In Effect: A SWOT analysis provides a comprehensive overview of an organisation's current standing, empowering it to make informed decisions about strategy, resource allocation, and risk management. By evaluating both internal and external factors, organisations gain clarity on how to leverage strengths and address weaknesses and threats.

SOAR Analysis

Strengths
- Like in SWOT analysis, SOAR underscores recognising and building upon an organisation's internal strengths and competitive advantages. This involves a

detailed exploration of what an organisation excels at and how it can leverage those strengths.

Opportunities
- In SOAR analysis, the primary focus is on exploring and maximising future opportunities. Rather than dwelling on threats, this approach encourages organisations/individuals to identify potential growth areas, emerging markets, and strategic alliances that can propel them forward.

Aspirations
- This distinctive aspect of SOAR involves envisioning and defining the desired future state or strategic goals of the organisation. By setting ambitious yet achievable aspirations, organisations inspire action and motivate employees towards a shared vision.

Results
- SOAR analysis places significant emphasis on tracking and measuring progress towards achieving desired outcomes. It entails defining and monitoring key performance indicators (KPIs) to ensure that the organisation is making meaningful strides towards its goals.

In Effect: SOAR analysis fosters a strengths-based approach to strategic planning. By accentuating what an organisation excels at and envisioning a positive future, it encourages proactive steps towards growth and success, while maintaining a forward-looking perspective.

6.2.4 Assess own skills against those required for a career in cyber security.

Embarking on a career in cybersecurity demands a comprehensive understanding of the skills and competencies vital for success in this dynamic field. To accurately assess your own skills in relation to the requisites of a cybersecurity profession, follow these structured steps:

1. **Review Job Descriptions**

    Initiate your assessment by immersing yourself in a thorough examination of job descriptions pertaining to cybersecurity roles that pique your interest. Scrutinise these postings for recurring themes in terms of skills and qualifications. Be attentive to the amalgamation of technical proficiencies and non-technical skills that employers are seeking.

2. **Identify Core Competencies**

    Drawing from the insights garnered from job descriptions and industry benchmarks, pinpoint the foundational competencies and skills indispensable for roles in cybersecurity. These may encompass technical proficiencies like network security, vulnerability assessment, or incident response, alongside non-technical proficiencies such as communication, problem-solving, and teamwork.

3. **Self-Assessment**

    Undertake a comprehensive self-assessment, critically evaluating your existing skills vis-à-vis the identified core competencies. Delve into your reservoir of knowledge, prior experiences, and level of proficiency in each skill domain. Foster an environment of Openness and introspection and conjure practical instances wherein you've demonstrated these proficiencies in the past.

4. **Seek Feedback**

    Broaden your perspective by soliciting feedback from seasoned professionals entrenched in the cybersecurity realm or from mentors who can proffer an objective evaluation of your skills. Articulate your self-assessment findings and implore them for their insights regarding your strengths and areas that may necessitate refinement. The constructive feedback they furnish can serve as a pivotal guidepost.

5. **Compare Skill Gaps**

    Execute a comparative analysis between the skills you've identified and the outcomes of your self-assessment. Discern the fissures that emerge between your extant skill set and the proficiencies mandated for cybersecurity roles. This meticulous scrutiny will furnish you with lucidity concerning the areas necessitating further cultivation and augmentation.

6. **Training and Education**

    Pore over a plethora of training programs, certifications, or educational prospects tailored to empower you in bridging these skill gaps. Seek out reputable courses, online platforms, workshops, or degree programs that are expressly designed to impart the requisite knowledge and skills pivotal in the cybersecurity domain.

7. **Practical Experience**

    Actively pursue opportunities to amass practical experience within the realm of cybersecurity. This can encompass internships, voluntary engagements, or endeavours on personal projects. Practical exposure not only affords you the platform to actualise your theoretical knowledge but also facilitates skill development and culminates in the creation of a portfolio that bears testimony to your proficiencies.

8. **Continuous Learning**

    The domain of cybersecurity is characterised by incessant evolution. To this end, commit resolutely to a regimen of perpetual learning. Stay abreast of the latest industry trends, emergent threats, and technological advancements. Engage actively in professional communities, attend conferences, participate in webinars, and devour pertinent literature to sustain your proficiency.

9. **Networking**

    Forge meaningful connections with stalwarts in the cybersecurity sphere. Immerse yourself in cybersecurity communities, partake in industry events, and engage in pertinent online forums or social media groups. Networking not only avails you of invaluable insights and mentorship prospects but also widens the gateway to potential job openings.

10. **Set Goals and Track Progress**

    Choreograph a meticulously detailed plan replete with specific goals and corresponding timelines for the acquisition or refinement of the requisite skills. Break down this plan into actionable steps and monitor your progress with unwavering regularity. Keep a meticulous record of your accomplishments, certifications, and practical experiences as tangible testaments to your ongoing growth.

Cybersecurity encompasses a vast array of specialisations. Tailor your skill acquisition efforts in alignment with your career aspirations and interests. Uphold the practice of periodic self-assessment and stay diligent in updating your skills inventory as you accrue experience and amass new proficiencies within the domain of cybersecurity.

Tutorial Activity - Multiple-choice Quiz

These questions cover various aspects of performing a personal skills analysis and assessing skills required for a career in cybersecurity:
1. Question: What is the first step in performing a personal skills analysis?

    1. a) Solicit Feedback

2. b) Create a Comprehensive Skills List

3. c) Review Job Descriptions

4. d) Identify the Purpose

2. Question: What should individuals do after identifying their strengths and weaknesses in a personal skills analysis?

   1. a) Craft an Action Plan

   2. b) Solicit Feedback

   3. c) Engage in Self-Reflection

   4. d) Spot Skill Gaps

3. Question: Which analysis emphasizes identifying strengths, weaknesses, opportunities, and threats?

   1. a) SWOT Analysis

   2. b) SOAR Analysis

   3. c) Personal Skills Analysis

   4. d) Skill Gap Analysis

4. Question: In SOAR analysis, what does "R" stand for?

   1. a) Risks

   2. b) Results

   3. c) Reflection

   4. d) Recognition

5. Question: What is the primary focus of SOAR analysis?

   1. a) Identifying weaknesses

   2. b) Exploring opportunities

   3. c) Assessing threats

   4. d) Recognising achievements

6. Question: What is the first step in assessing one's skills against those required for a career in cybersecurity?

1. a) Seek Feedback
2. b) Identify Core Competencies
3. c) Review Job Descriptions
4. d) Self-Assessment

7. Question: What should individuals do after identifying skill gaps for a career in cybersecurity?

    1. a) Seek Feedback
    2. b) Training and Education
    3. c) Continuous Learning
    4. d) Networking

8. Question: What is emphasized in the section about assessing own skills against those required for a career in cybersecurity?

    1. a) Practical Experience
    2. b) Setting Goals and Tracking Progress
    3. c) Continuous Learning
    4. d) All of the above

9. Question: What should individuals do after creating a comprehensive skills list in a personal skills analysis?

    1. a) Solicit Feedback
    2. b) Engage in Self-Reflection
    3. c) Seek Feedback
    4. d) Identify Core Competencies

10. Question: What is the final step recommended in assessing one's skills for a career in cybersecurity?

    1. a) Setting Goals and Tracking Progress
    2. b) Self-Assessment
    3. c) Reviewing Job Descriptions

4. d) Continuous Learning

6.2.5 Create a Personal Development Plan

A personal development plan serves as a compass, guiding individuals towards their goals while highlighting areas for improvement and delineating the necessary steps for achievement. Below is a detailed guide for producing a robust personal development plan:

1. **Set Clear Goals**

Embark on your personal development journey by elucidating your overarching personal and professional objectives. These goals should be SMART: Specific, Measurable, Achievable, Relevant, and Time-bound. Ensuring specificity and measurability empowers you to gauge progress effectively.

2. **Conduct a Self-Assessment**

Undertake a comprehensive self-assessment, unearthing your existing strengths, areas for improvement, and latent potential. This entails a deep dive into your skills, knowledge, experiences, and innate attributes. Identify the facets that harmonise with your aspirations and the competencies necessitating refinement.

3. **Prioritise Areas for Development**

In light of your self-assessment outcomes and the goals you have delineated, give precedence to the areas warranting development. Concentrate on skills and competencies poised to wield the most substantial influence on your personal and professional evolution.

4. **Research Development Opportunities**

Survey the expansive landscape of resources and opportunities available to bolster your chosen skills. This can encompass an array of options, spanning formal avenues like training programs, workshops, and courses, to informal channels such as online platforms, books, mentorship, and engagement with professional associations.

5. **Set Actionable Steps**

Translate your development goals into tangible, actionable steps or milestones. Determine the precise actions requisite for each goal's attainment. Be explicit and granular in specifying the measures you will take, whether it entails enrolling in a course, participating in a workshop, or culminating a project.

6. **Create a Timeline**

    Erect a structured timeline encompassing each step or milestone. Assign deadlines to galvanise your commitment and maintain momentum. Factor in the duration required for each developmental endeavour and integrate it seamlessly into the broader framework of your personal development plan.

7. **Seek Support and Guidance**

    Identify individuals who can furnish invaluable support throughout your personal development expedition. This cohort may comprise mentors, coaches, colleagues, or seasoned professionals within your target domain. Seek their sagacity, counsel, and feedback, leveraging their expertise to fortify your progress.

8. **Take Action**

    Commence the execution of your personal development plan by initiating the essential actions stipulated in each step. Begin with the inaugural milestone and proceed with methodical precision. Uphold a steadfast resolve and unwavering dedication to your plan, monitoring your advancement at every juncture.

9. **Reflect and Evaluate**

    Punctuate your journey with regular moments of reflection and evaluation. Deliberate upon your progress, discerning what is functioning optimally and where refinements are warranted. Effectuate revisions to your plan as necessitated, acclimating it to novel opportunities, challenges, or shifts in your aspirations.

10. **Celebrate Achievements**

    Celebrate your accomplishments, regardless of their magnitude, along the trajectory of your development. Acknowledge the strides you've made and the milestones you've achieved. The act of commemorating these victories, however small, serves as a potent motivator, kindling the impetus for further growth.

Bear in mind that a personal development plan is a malleable document, amenable to adjustment and augmentation as you progress and confront fresh opportunities. Consistently scrutinise your goals, fine-tune your plan, and remain receptive to learning and development throughout the entirety of your personal and professional odyssey.

Tutorial Activity - Multiple-choice Quiz

6.2.5 Tutorial Quiz:

Quiz 1: Set Clear Goals

What does SMART stand for in the context of setting clear goals?

    a) Specific, Measured, Achievable, Realistic, Time-bound

    b) Specific, Measurable, Achievable, Relevant, Time-bound

    c) Strategic, Measurable, Achievable, Relevant, Timely

    d) Specific, Measurable, Actionable, Relevant, Timely

Quiz 2: Conduct a Self-Assessment

What does a comprehensive self-assessment involve?

    a) Analysing only existing strengths

    b) Identifying only areas for improvement

    c) Evaluating skills, knowledge, experiences, and innate attributes

    d) Focusing solely on professional aspirations

Quiz 3: Prioritise Areas for Development

Why is it important to prioritise areas for development?

    a) To avoid any self-assessment

    b) To focus on irrelevant skills

    c) To concentrate on skills and competencies with the most impact

    d) To ignore personal and professional goals

Quiz 4: Create a Timeline

What is the purpose of creating a timeline in a personal development plan?

    a) To make the plan confusing

    b) To assign deadlines and maintain momentum

    c) To disregard deadlines and milestones

    d) To ignore the duration required for developmental endeavours

Quiz 5: Seek Support and Guidance

Who can provide invaluable support during your personal development journey?

a) Only colleagues

b) Only mentors

c) Only professional associations

d) Mentors, coaches, colleagues, or seasoned professionals within your target domain

6.3 Continuous Professional Development (CPD)

Continuous Professional Development (CPD) is a dynamic and purposeful process that entails actively seeking out opportunities to enhance one's professional knowledge, skills, and competencies throughout the entirety of their career journey. It transcends the realm of initial education and formal qualifications, acknowledging that professionals must perpetually learn, adapt, and evolve to remain adept and proficient in their respective domains. At its core, CPD is a proactive approach to professional development that advocates for lifelong learning and ensures that professionals remain equipped with the most up-to-date knowledge and skills pertinent to their field.

6.3.1 Key Principles of CPD

1. **Lifelong Learning:** CPD places paramount importance on the notion of perpetual learning throughout one's professional trajectory. It operates on the premise that knowledge and skills undergo a natural process of evolution and obsolescence, necessitating a continuous commitment to staying abreast of emerging developments and evolving trends within the industry.

2. **Reflective Practice:** CPD encourages individuals to engage in reflective practices, which involves introspection and self-assessment of one's professional performance. This introspective process enables professionals to discern areas warranting refinement, seek constructive feedback from peers or mentors, and engage in a critical analysis of their own competencies and contributions.

3. **Varied Learning Activities:** CPD is an all-encompassing endeavour that encompasses a diverse array of learning activities and experiences. These activities can span a spectrum, including participation in conferences, attendance at workshops and seminars, pursuit of advanced education or specialised certifications, engagement in online courses, active involvement in professional associations, perusal of industry-related publications, and cultivation of mentoring or coaching relationships.

4. **Personalised Development Plans:** A pivotal facet of CPD entails the creation of personalised development plans tailored to individualised professional aspirations, goals, and areas necessitating enhancement. This bespoke approach enables professionals to tailor their learning activities and experiences to their specific needs and aspirations, ensuring that their professional development aligns with their unique trajectory.

5. **Tracking and Documentation:** CPD mandates that professionals diligently track and document their learning activities and accomplishments. This may encompass the maintenance of a comprehensive CPD portfolio, meticulous recording of completed courses or training programs, collection of relevant certifications, and vigilant documentation of professional achievements.

6.3.2 Benefits of CPD

1. **Enhanced Professional Competence:** CPD stands as a testament to a professional's unwavering commitment to staying at the vanguard of their field. By consistently integrating the latest knowledge, techniques, and practices into their repertoire, professionals bolster their competence, equipping them to deliver superlative services and remain pertinent in an ever-evolving professional landscape.

2. **Career Advancement:** Active participation in CPD activities can be instrumental in fostering career progression and advancement. It serves as a tangible demonstration of one's dedication to ongoing learning and professional development, a quality highly esteemed by employers. This commitment can unlock new avenues and opportunities for growth.

3. **Networking and Collaboration:** CPD activities frequently serve as conduits for interactions with peers, subject matter experts, and professionals from diverse organisations. These interactions create fertile ground for networking, knowledge exchange, and collaborative ventures, fostering the development of professional relationships and broadening one's network within the industry.

4. **Personal Fulfilment:** The pursuit of continuous learning and growth can bestow a profound sense of personal fulfilment and gratification. It empowers professionals to venture into uncharted territories, explore new realms of interest, confront intellectual challenges, and ultimately, cultivate a profound sense of accomplishment.

CPD stands as an integral cornerstone of a professional's journey, offering a structured framework for sustained growth and evolution. It is a testament to the professional's unwavering commitment to excellence, a commitment that ensures they remain dynamic, proficient, and ready to meet the evolving demands of their field.

6.3.3 Methods of Keeping Up to Date with Industry Knowledge

Staying abreast of industry knowledge is an indispensable practice for professionals seeking to remain at the forefront of their respective fields. The dynamic nature of industries demands a proactive approach to learning and an unwavering commitment to ongoing education. Here are comprehensive methods to ensure you are consistently informed and updated:

1. **Professional Associations and Organisations**

Joining professional associations and organisations closely aligned with your industry provides an invaluable gateway to a wealth of industry-specific resources. Membership often grants access to a plethora of benefits including newsletters, publications, webinars, conferences, and networking events. These platforms serve as conduits for staying informed of the latest trends, innovations, and developments within the industry.

2. **Industry Publications and Journals**

Subscribing to industry-specific publications, magazines, journals, and newsletters is a cornerstone of remaining informed about the most recent advancements in your field. These sources offer in-depth analysis, research findings, case studies, and expert perspectives, furnishing you with a comprehensive understanding of industry trends, emerging technologies, and best practices.

3. **Online Resources and Websites**

Leverage the power of online resources by frequenting industry-specific websites, blogs, forums, and news aggregators. These digital platforms serve as hubs for timely articles, blog posts, discussion forums, and curated news items that are pivotal in keeping you apprised of the latest industry developments. Additionally, following influential thought leaders and subject matter experts on social media platforms can provide an additional stream of insights.

4. **Webinars and Online Courses**

Attend webinars and participate in online courses that are directly pertinent to your industry. Webinars offer the unique opportunity to glean insights from subject matter experts, providing unparalleled access to emerging trends and technologies. Online courses, on the other hand, deliver structured learning experiences that can serve to deepen your proficiency in specific areas of interest.

5. **Conferences and Events**

Actively participate in industry conferences, seminars, workshops, and trade shows. These gatherings serve as epicentres for the convergence of professionals, thought leaders, and experts across various sectors of your industry. They furnish you with the exclusive opportunity to learn, network, and gain firsthand exposure to the latest advancements, breakthroughs, and industry practices.

6. **Networking and Professional Communities**

Engage in robust networking activities and become a part of professional communities, both in the virtual and physical realms. Immersing yourself in industry-specific LinkedIn groups, online forums, and social media communities allows for meaningful engagement with peers, experts, and professionals. These interactions facilitate valuable knowledge sharing, vibrant discussions, and the exchange of insightful perspectives.

7. **Mentorship and Coaching**

Actively seek out mentorship or coaching relationships with seasoned professionals possessing extensive experience and knowledge within your industry. These mentors serve as invaluable sources of guidance, repositories of wisdom, and conduits to staying updated on the most current industry trends. Regular meetings and discussions with mentors offer profound learning experiences that are invaluable in professional growth.

8. **Continuous Learning Platforms**

Harness the potential of online learning platforms like Udemy, Coursera, LinkedIn Learning, and Pluralsight. These platforms provide an extensive array of courses and learning resources spanning a diverse spectrum of topics, including those specific to your industry. Engaging with these platforms empowers you to acquire and refine industry-relevant skills and knowledge.

9. **Podcasts and Audiobooks**

Optimise your commute or leisure time by immersing yourself in industry-related podcasts and audiobooks. Podcasts frequently feature interviews with experts, thought-provoking discussions, and comprehensive explorations of industry trends. Audiobooks, on the other hand, offer deep dives into specific subjects, furnishing you with a profound understanding of pertinent topics.

10. **Industry Events and Webcasts**

Remain vigilant about upcoming industry events, webcasts, and online seminars. These forums frequently showcase industry leaders, keynote speakers, and panel discussions on current topics and trends. Participation in these events is invaluable in gaining insights and perspectives from luminaries within the field.

Remember to allocate dedicated time for continuous learning and to set aside regular intervals to review and update your industry knowledge. Actively seek out opportunities to learn, engage with the community, and remain curious about emerging trends and developments. This steadfast commitment to professional development will serve as a cornerstone in your ongoing success and growth within the industry.

6.3.4 Importance of Keeping Continuous Professional Development (CPD) Up to Date

Ensuring that Continuous Professional Development (CPD) remains current is pivotal for a multitude of compelling reasons:

1. **Stay Current with Industry Trends**

Industries are dynamic, perpetually shaped by technological advancements, shifting regulatory landscapes, and the emergence of innovative best practices. Engaging in CPD empowers professionals to keep abreast of the latest trends, cutting-edge innovations, and progressive developments within their field. This knowledge equips them to seamlessly adapt to industry changes and maintain a competitive edge.

2. **Enhance Professional Competence**

CPD serves as an instrumental conduit for professionals to amplify their proficiency, expertise, and competency levels. Through active participation in learning endeavours, professionals can deepen their subject matter expertise, acquire novel skills, and refine existing ones. This elevated level of professional competence translates to heightened effectiveness and efficiency in their roles.

3. **Meet Regulatory and Compliance Requirements**

Numerous professions are subject to oversight by regulatory bodies or licensing authorities, mandating professionals to engage in CPD as a prerequisite to preserve their accreditation or licenses. Synchronising CPD initiatives with regulatory demands ensures compliance, sidestepping potential penalties or jeopardising one's professional standing.

4. **Deliver High-Quality Services**

CPD serves as a pivotal mechanism to equip professionals with the latest knowledge and optimal practices, arming them to deliver superlative services to their clients, customers, or stakeholders. By remaining current, professionals can furnish precise, pertinent, and efficacious solutions, guaranteeing optimal outcomes for their clients or organisations.

5. **Adapt to Technological Advancements**

Technology holds a pivotal role in shaping industries and professional landscapes. CPD is an indispensable instrument in enabling professionals to stay abreast of technological progressions germane to their domain. This equips them to leverage new tools, platforms, and methodologies, augmenting their efficiency, productivity, and proficiency in resolving challenges.

6. **Embrace Lifelong Learning**

CPD champions the ethos of perpetual learning, underscoring the significance of continuous evolution and enhancement. Professionals who immerse themselves in CPD exemplify a dedication to ongoing development, self-refinement, and personal maturation. This disposition nurtures a spirit of curiosity, adaptability, and resilience in the face of change.

7. **Career Advancement Opportunities**

CPD serves as a gateway to new vistas of career prospects and progression. Employers hold in high regard professionals who demonstrate an unwavering commitment to ongoing learning and development. By actively participating in CPD, professionals can expand their skill set, broaden their knowledge base, and heighten their marketability, augmenting their prospects for career advancement.

8. **Networking and Collaboration**

CPD pursuits frequently entail engagements with peers, luminaries, and professionals within the same industry or discipline. This engenders opportunities for networking, the exchange of knowledge, and the cultivation of collaborative endeavours. Nurturing relationships with fellow professionals can yield invaluable insights, avenues for mentorship, and potential collaborations.

9. **Personal Satisfaction and Motivation**

The engagement in CPD activities affords professionals the latitude to pursue their interests, nurture their passions, and cultivate personal growth. It engenders a sense of accomplishment, satisfaction, and motivation as individuals expand their knowledge base, attain personal milestones, and bear witness to the tangible impact of their development endeavours.

10. **Future-Proofing Careers**

In the face of rapid industry evolution, professionals who fail to prioritise CPD expose themselves to the risk of obsolescence and diminished relevance in the job market. By assiduously keeping CPD current, professionals immunise their careers against these perils. They proactively position themselves at the vanguard of industry shifts, perpetuate their employability, and assert themselves as invaluable assets to their organisations.

With these compelling reasons in mind, professionals are prompted to not only initiate CPD endeavours but also to diligently ensure their ongoing relevance and applicability in the professional sphere. This steadfast commitment to CPD will serve as an indelible cornerstone in their journey of sustained success and perpetual growth within their respective fields.

Tutorial Activity - Multiple-choice Quiz

6.3.4 Tutorial Quiz:

Quiz 1: Stay Current with Industry Trends

Why is engaging in Continuous Professional Development (CPD) important for professionals according to the text?

    a) To avoid industry trends

    b) To keep abreast of the latest trends and developments

    c) To remain stagnant in their careers

    d) To ignore technological advancements

Quiz 2: Enhance Professional Competence

How does CPD contribute to enhancing professional competence?

    a) By avoiding learning endeavours

b) By staying away from acquiring novel skills

c) By deepening subject matter expertise and acquiring new skills

d) By disregarding existing competencies

Quiz 3: Meet Regulatory and Compliance Requirements

Why do regulatory bodies mandate professionals to engage in CPD?

a) To ignore compliance requirements

b) To face potential penalties

c) To preserve their accreditation or licenses

d) To relinquish their professional standing

Quiz 4: Adapt to Technological Advancements

How does CPD help professionals adapt to technological advancements?

a) By ignoring technological progressions

b) By staying outdated in their domain

c) By staying abreast of technological progressions relevant to their domain

d) By avoiding new tools and methodologies

Quiz 5: Embrace Lifelong Learning

CPD champions what ethos?

a) Perpetual stagnation

b) Continuous evolution and enhancement

c) Avoidance of personal maturation

d) Temporary learning endeavours

www.ingramcontent.com/pod-product-compliance
Lightning Source LLC
Chambersburg PA
CBHW062103220526
45471CB00010B/3583